GW00802018

MACRAMÉ PATTERNS

MACRAMÉ PATTERNS

Kit Pyman

B T Batsford Limited London

ACKNOWLEDGMENT

I would like to say how grateful I am to three friends in particular for their professional contributions to this book.

To Jan Messent, for making clear diagrams out of my rough sketches and for the two pages of beautiful drawings, all worked with meticulous care and attention to detail.

To Roger Cuthbert for all the photography, for the time and skill taken to bring out the textures, and for his imaginative approach to the composition and lighting.

To Dot Milsted, for working and re-working the designs, and always with the greatest patience and good humour.

I would also like to thank Thelma Nye for kindly lending me a most inspirational butterfly, Jack Aldous of Atlas Handicrafts for generously giving most of the materials, and Mavis Waghorn for re-typing the text.

Finally, there are no words to express my gratitude to my husband for his support, forbearance and mathematical expertise on the conversion of imperial measurements to metric, so I shall just dedicate this book to him, with my love.

© Kit Pyman 1980
First published 1980

Printed and bound in Great Britain by
Butler Tanner Ltd, Frome, Somerset
for the publishers B.T. Batsford Limited
4 Fitzhardinge Street, London W1H 0AH

ISBN 0 7134 3307 8

CONTENTS

PREFACE

This book is divided into two parts. Part 1 is for beginners. There are four samplers to work through, teaching the basic knots of macramé — the half hitch, the half knot, the flat knot and cavandoli work. As well as the basic knots, their variations, and ways of combining them, the beginner will also learn points of technique and methods of working which speed up and simplify the knotting.

Experienced knotters will go straight to Part II, which gives patterns for upwards of fifty items. They may only wish to abstract the essential information — the type of yarn, the number of set-on threads and the lengths to cut — after which it is simply a matter of working from the photograph or developing one's own design.

The patterns are all based on the two macramé knots; the half hitch and the flat knot. Any unusual knots or techniques are explained and illustrated with the relevant text. If a beginner has worked through the samplers he or she will have no difficulty with the patterns, which are all based on these simple exercises.

Some sections of Part II are prefaced by general instructions for a particular technique — working fringes, or making 3D flowers, covering lampshade frames and planning cavandoli graphs — and they suggest methods of work, suitable yarns, required lengths, and ideas for variations on the basic design.

Measurements are given in both Metric and Imperial, the basic unit being 2.5 cm which equals approximately 1 in.

Yarns are mentioned by name if they are a commercial product, or by a general term such as string, wool, jute — when no particular yarn is specified. One of the main reasons for a failure with a pattern is the substitution of another yarn, and for this reason the 'size' of a yarn is given in millimetres, the width measured across the thread with a ruler. An approximate imperial equivalent of these measurements has also been supplied. A section called Notes on Yarns on page 117 describes the yarns recommended and the list of suppliers will enable the reader to locate where they are available.

Part 1

TECHNIQUES

THE SAMPLERS

The first sampler teaches the half hitch, the second the half knot, and the third the flat knot, and how to combine this with the other two knots. The fourth sampler is cavandoli work, not the traditional macramé, but a particular form of close knotting with many interesting uses.

To work the samplers the following equipment is recommended:·

A knotting board This could be a piece of fibre board, soft board or insulating board, or an old cork bathmat, or a padded sheet of card. It should be soft enough to hold pins, and rigid enough to balance on the knees at an angle, and ideally should not measure less than 30 cm (12 in.) by 38 cm (15 in.).

Pins Use the large T-pins supplied for the purpose. They are strong enough to tension the threads and anchor the work in progress. Dressmakers' pins are used to secure headings, and often replace T-pins as the work progresses, as they can be pushed in up to the heads and will not tangle in the knotting. Ten pins of each type will be enough to work the samplers.

A ball of string A fine hemp twine measuring 1 mm ($^1/_{16}$ in.) across was used for the samplers. Each sampler uses about 7.5 m (8 yd) of string.

A bulldog clip or twisted wire hook Some method of keeping the threads taut is needed, so that the hands are free for knotting. Both methods are described in Sampler 2.

Scissors An ordinary medium-sized pair will do.

Preparation Mark out the knotting board in 2.5 cm (1 in.) squares, with a ballpoint pen. This grid enables the horizontal and diagonal lines of the sampler to be positioned accurately, and can also be used as a measure.

Sit in an upright chair with one end of the board on the knees and the other propped against a table. This gives an inclined work surface which is comfortable, and later on essential when taut threads have to be secured to a clip at the waist.

Arrange the scissors, T-pins, small pins and the ball of string within reach.

Start the sampler half-way down the board, as shown in the sketch, so that the knotting is within easy reach of the fingers.

1 Working position

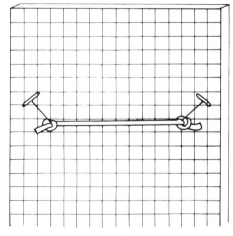

2 Mounting a holding cord

Cut six 120 cm (4 ft) lengths of string. As a general rule, the length of threads should be eight times the length of the finished article (four times when doubled). As the first sampler is about 15 cm (6 in.) long, the cut lengths will be eight times that measurement.

Starting a Sampler
All the samplers are set up in the same way, following figures 1 to 5.

Cut
Six 120 cm (4 ft) lengths.

3 The overhand knot

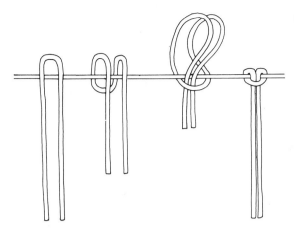

4 Setting on a doubled thread with lark's head knot

Mount a holding card Cut a 20 cm (8 in.) length of string, make an overhand knot each end. Fix the string taut across the board halfway down, pushing a T-pin (sloping outwards to take the strain) through the knots.

Set on a thread Double one length, and set it on to the holding cord with a lark's head knot as shown in figure 4.

Set on a row of threads Set on the five remaining lengths in the same way, and arrange the knots side by side in a neat row.

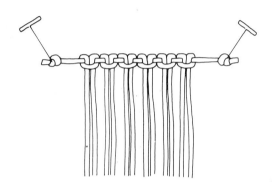

5 A row of six set-on threads

Sampler 1 THE HALF HITCH

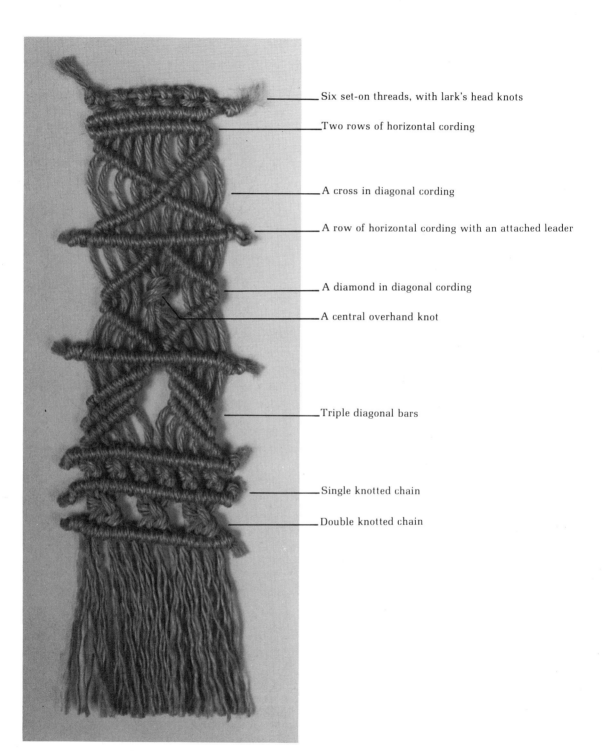

Six set-on threads, with lark's head knots

Two rows of horizontal cording

A cross in diagonal cording

A row of horizontal cording with an attached leader

A diamond in diagonal cording

A central overhand knot

Triple diagonal bars

Single knotted chain

Double knotted chain

The most common use of this knot is in cording, which makes the horizontal and diagonal bars which are so characteristic of macramé work. These bars consist of double half hitches knotted over a taut thread. Macramé knots are not tied like parcel knots, with both threads being entwined, but are tied with a 'knotting' thread over a taut passive thread. (The holding cord is one of these passive threads, held taut by pins, and it carries the set-on threads.)

Cording is worked with the 'knotting' threads over a thread held taut in the hand called the 'leader'. The corded bar will lie in any direction in which the leader is held — if it is held straight across the work the result will be a bar of horizontal cording, and if it is held slanting then the result will be a bar of diagonal cording. This leader can also be held in different directions to form curves and wriggles. It can consist of one of the threads belonging to the work on hand, or another sort of yarn altogether, or a bunch of yarn, or something rigid like a stick, or a solid shape like a fan belt, or anything else you like to use.

The following sampler teaches the use of double half hitches in making corded bars from right to left, left to right, and diagonally, using an integral thread and an attached leader.

Work a row of horizontal cording from right to left
Stick in a T-pin between the last two threads, just below the last lark's head knot. Slope the pin outwards to stand the strain. Pick up the

last thread in the left hand and hold it horizontally across the board, parallel to the holding cord. This is the leader. Keep it taut. Now pick up the last (eleventh) thread in the right hand and loop it over the leader in a clockwise direction. Pull the loop tight, push it along the leader until it is directly under the last lark's head knot. This is a half hitch.

Make another half hitch with the *same* thread over the leader in the same way. This makes a double half hitch. Tighten it, push it along the leader beside the first half hitch. You will notice that one half hitch merely makes a loop over the leader, whereas a second one turns it into a secure knot. Cording is always worked with double half hitches, never with single ones.

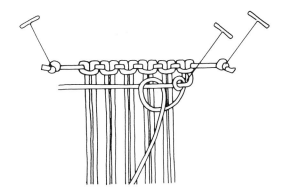

7 Making a double half hitch on a leader

Pick up the next (tenth) thread, and with it make another double half hitch on to the leader. Put a pin into the lark's head knot belonging to these two threads which have been knotted on to the leader. Continue across the work, picking up each thread in turn and making a double half hitch on to the leader, until there is a firm knotted bar lying parallel to the holding cord, and all the lark's head knots are pinned into place. Don't pin the lark's heads before their two threads are knotted on to the leader, and check that they are in line on the grid.

Beginner's mistakes If the bar slopes to the left, it may be that you were so busy

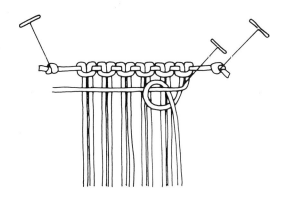

6 Making a half hitch on a leader

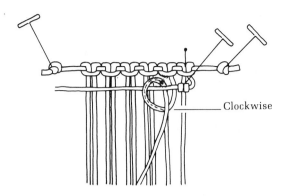

8 Working a row of horizontal cording from right to left

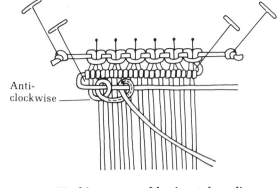

9 Working a row of horizontal cording from left to right

making the knots that the leader was not held taut and horizontal — if the leader sags in the middle so will the bar. If the loops look untidy, did you pull each knot firmly and push it along beside the previous one? Did you remember to make a *double* half hitch every time with each thread? You should be able to count 22 little loops across the bar.

Don't undo the bar if it is not perfect, it is only a practice sampler, so go on to the next stage.

Work a row of horizontal cording from left to right

The same leader is used. Stick in a T-pin (sloping outwards to take the strain) just below the first lark's head knot under the leader. Turn the leader round it, and hold it taut in the right hand across the work, parallel to the first row of cording. Going this way, the loops of the half hitch go anti-clockwise instead of clockwise. Pick up the first thread in the left hand (try to get used to this two-handed approach) and loop it anti-clockwise over the leader in the first half hitch. Push the loop along the leader, make a second half hitch in the same way with the same thread, and push it alongside the first. Pull firmly. Keep the leader taut. Continue across the row making double half hitches over the leader with each thread in turn.

Now that the heading is secured with small pins, the T-pins at the ends of the holding

cord can be taken out. T-pins are necessary to take the weight of the work and the pull of the leader threads, but they can be removed or replaced with small pins as the work progresses. Think of macramé as if it were lace — it needs to be pinned in place as it progresses, but the pins can be small and embedded in the soft knotting board at sharp angles so that they don't get tangled in the working threads.

Make a cross in diagonal cording

Move the left-hand T-pin down so that it is between the first and second threads, sloping outwards. The first thread is going to be a new leader — hold it taut in the right hand diagonally across the work to the right. Pick up the second thread with the left hand and make a double half hitch on to the leader (remember to make the loop anti-clockwise). Work a double half hitch on to the leader with the next five threads.

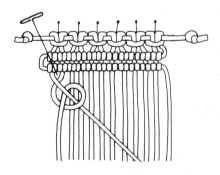

10 Working a row of diagonal cording from left to right

Leave these six threads aside for the moment, and work the other diagonal bar. Stick in a T-pin just under the last (twelfth) thread, slopping outwards. Turn the thread round the pin and hold it taut diagonally across the work with the left hand. This leader should be aimed to the point where the arm of the cross is to finish, with the help of the grid. Using the right hand, make a row of double half hitches over the leader with each thread in turn right across the work, *including* the previous leader now hanging in the middle. Secure the bar with a small pin.

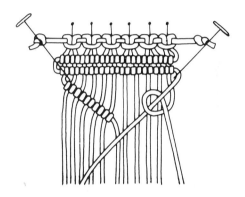

11 Working a row of diagonal cording from right to left

Complete cross by using seventh thread as leader, holding it diagonally to the right with the right hand, and making a double half hitch on to it with each of the remaining five threads in turn. Pin this bar in place also.

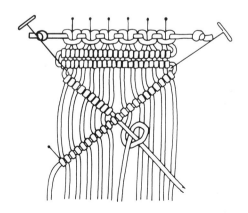

12 Completing a cross in diagonal cording

How to use an attached leader
Up to now an integral thread has been used as a leader. Learn to use an 'attached' leader, which is a separate length of yarn brought in for this purpose. Cut a 20 cm (8 in.) length of string, make an overhand knot at one end, pin the knot to the board on the right of the sampler where the horizontal bar is to lie. Using this 'attached leader' make a row of horizontal cording from right to left over all threads. At the end of the row, loop the leader out of the way. When the work is finished, this end is either sewn into the back, or knotted close to the work and cut.

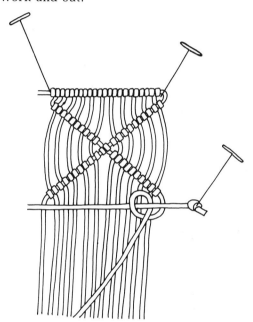

13 Working a row of cording with an attached leader

Make a diamond in diagonal cording
Locate the two centre threads and, using them as leaders, cord them out to left and right diagonally over the remaining threads.

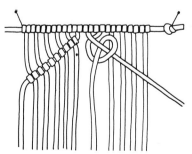

14 The first half of a diamond in diagonal cording

Central knot This is an overhand knot (figure 3) made with the central four threads. Keep the knot loose until it is correctly positioned, then tighten and secure with a small pin.

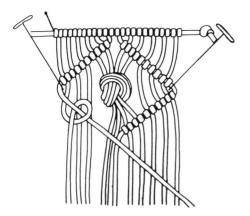

15 Completing a diamond in diagonal cording

Complete diamond by placing T-pins at the sides just within the two leaders, bending the leaders round the pins, and cording back into the centre.

Make another row of horizontal cording with an attached leader. Left-handed knotters may find it easier to work from left to right, pinning the leader to the left of the work.

Triple diagonal bars
Rows of diagonal cording may be worked in any direction. To make the chevron shape in figure 16, cord out from the centre as in figure 14 three times. Note that the leader of one row is left hanging in place to become a

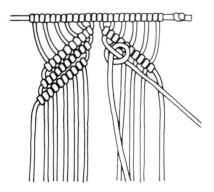

16 Three rows of diagonal cording

knotting thread in the next row. Diamonds and crosses may be worked in double or triple rows of cording in this way.

Work another row of horizontal cording with an attached leader.

Vertical half hitches
Another way of using the half hitch is vertically instead of horizontally. Knotted chain is not worked with a single leader like cording, but with pairs of threads which take turns to be leader.

Single knotted chain
This is worked with pairs of threads across the row. Take the first thread of the sampler and hold it taut in the left hand. Hold the second thread in the right hand and make a half hitch on to the first thread, as in figure 17. The first thread is the leader and the second thread is the knotting thread. Now change the leader, hold the

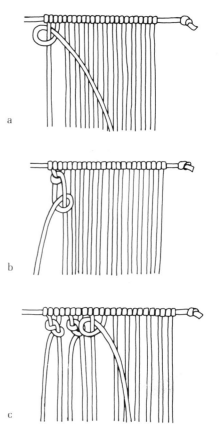

17 Single knotted chain

16

second thread taut, and make a half hitch on to it with the first (now knotting) thread. Don't change hands, don't tie the knot with both hands, but work consciously with one taut thread and one knotting thread. One half hitch to the left, as in (a), followed by one half hitch to the right, as in (b), results in one single knotted chain.

Work right across the row, making one single knotted chain with each pair of threads, as in (c).

With an attached leader, work a row of horizontal cording.

Double knotted chain is exactly the same as single knotted chain, except that it is worked with two threads in each hand — the 'double' referring to the number of threads and not to the number of knots.

Divide the threads into groups of four, and work one double knotted chain on each group across the row, as in figure 18 (a) (b) and (c).

Finish off the sampler by working another row of horizontal cording with an attached leader. Cut the ends about 5 cm (2 in.) below the cording, and fray them out into a fringe.

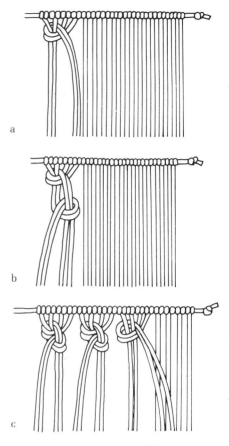

18 Double knotted chain

Sampler 2 THE HALF KNOT

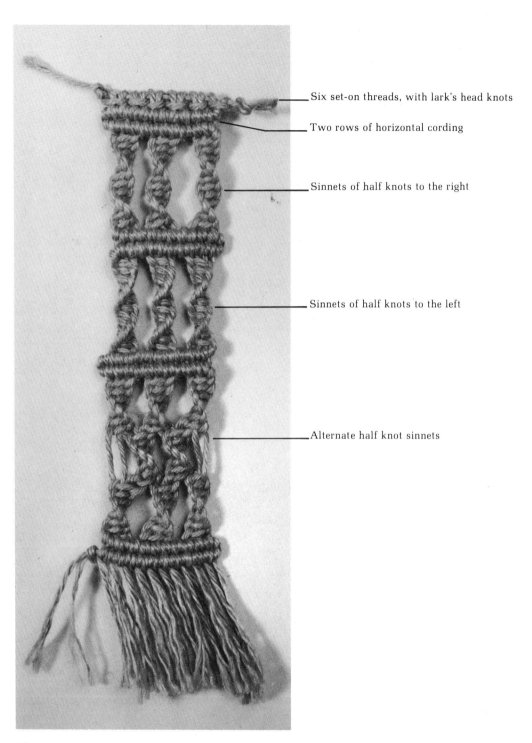

Six set-on threads, with lark's head knots

Two rows of horizontal cording

Sinnets of half knots to the right

Sinnets of half knots to the left

Alternate half knot sinnets

The half knot is made with four threads, and a series of them makes a spiral sinnet. A sinnet is a nautical term, meaning a narrow length of knotting. In the first section of the sampler the half knot sinnets spiral to the right, in the second section they spiral to the left, and in the last section they are worked into a pattern of alternate half knot sinnets. Each section is divided by two rows of horizontal cording.

The central threads of any sinnet are held taut. They are another example of taut threads which are knotted *over*, like holding cords and leaders. The central threads of a sinnet are called core threads (or filler cords, or foundation threads, or anchor cords) and the outer threads which make the knots are called knotting threads (or working cords). But whereas the holding cord is fixed to the board, and the leader is held in the hand, some method has to be found of keeping the core threads taut while both hands are making the knots.

19 Keeping the core threads taut

One method is to tie a bulldog clip round the waist and grip the core threads in this, as shown in the sketch, and another method is to use a sailor's hook, shown in figure 20, and wind the core threads round it twice, as shown, so that they are held taut while the knot is made. This is a much quicker method than clipping and unclipping threads from a bulldog clip, once the knack of hitching the threads onto the hook is learned.

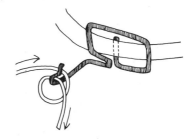

20 A macramé hook

Set up the sampler in exactly the same way as the first, as far as figure 9, with rows of horizontal cording. Make sure the set-on threads are firmly pinned to the board.

A sinnet of half knots spiralling to the right
Use the first group of four threads. Grip the two core threads in the clip or wind them over the hook, so that they are held taut.

Lay the first thread across to the right *over* the core threads and under the fourth thread. (The first and fourth threads are the knotting threads).

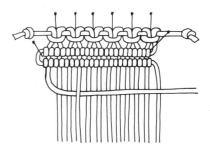

21a Making a half knot to the right, stage 1

Pass the fourth thread *under* the two core threads and *over* the first thread.

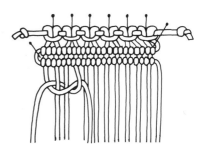

21b Making a half knot to the right, stage 2

Pull the knotting threads and run the knot up to the row of cording and make it firm — this is a half knot to the right.

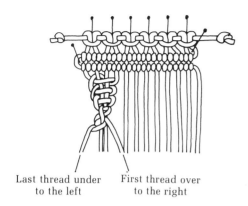

Last thread under to the left   First thread over to the right

22 A half-knot sinnet spiralling to the right

Make three more half knots. At this point you will find the sinnet beginning to twist to the right.

If it is not doing so, have you made the knot the right way? Have you pulled each knot firmly and pushed it up tightly against the previous one?

When the sinnet turns, lay the first thread *over* the core threads to the right, and bring the fourth thread *under* the core threads to the left. As the sinnet spirals, the knotting threads change places. Work six more half knots, during which the sinnet will spiral once more. Move on to the next group of four threads, and work ten half knots. Make ten half knots on the last group of four threads.

Pin each sinnet in place as it is completed. Using the first thread as leader, work two rows of horizontal cording.

A sinnet of half knots spiralling to the left
Use the first group of four threads, keep the two core threads taut, and lay the fourth thread to the left over the core threads and under the first thread.

Pass the first thread under the two core threads and over the fourth thread. Push the

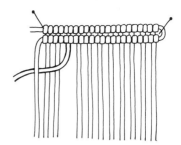

23a Making a half knot to the left, stage 1

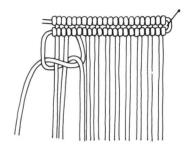

23b Making a half knot to the left, stage 2

knot up to the cording and make it firm. This is a half knot to the left.

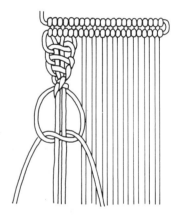

24 A half knot sinnet spiralling to the left

Make three more half knots to the left, and when the sinnet begins to turn to the left, bring the fourth thread over the core to the left, and pass the first thread under the core to the right, thus changing over the knotting threads. Work six more half knots, during which the sinnet will spiral once more. Pin sinnet in place. Make ten half knots to the left on each of the two remaining groups of four threads, completing three half knot sinnets. Pin the other two sinnets in place.

Using the last thread as leader, make two rows of horizontal cording.

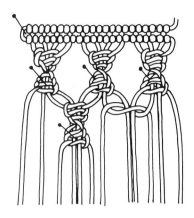

25 Alternate half knot sinnets

Alternate half knot sinnets
Row 1 — Divide threads as before into groups of four. Work seven half knots to the right in each group. Pin each sinnet in place as it is completed. Each sinnet should spiral once.

Row 2 — Leave first two and last two threads idle. Re-divide remaining threads into groups of four. On each group work seven half knots to the right. Pin each sinnet in place as it is completed.

Repeat Row 1 once.

To finish
Using the first thread as leader, work two rows of horizontal cording. Cut ends 2.5 cm (1 in.) below the last row of cording, and fray them out to make a fringe.

Sampler 3   THE FLAT KNOT

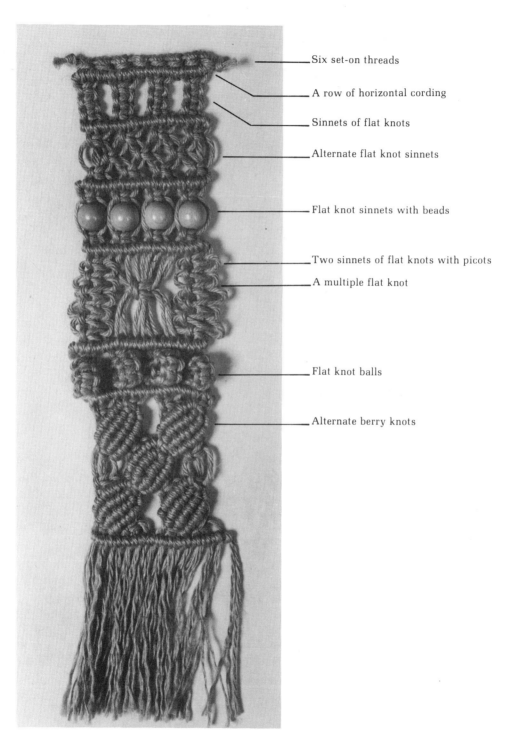

Six set-on threads

A row of horizontal cording

Sinnets of flat knots

Alternate flat knot sinnets

Flat knot sinnets with beads

Two sinnets of flat knots with picots

A multiple flat knot

Flat knot balls

Alternate berry knots

The flat knot or square knot consists of two half knots, one to the right and one to the left. A sinnet of half knots will always spiral, whereas a sinnet of flat knots lies flat. The flat knot is capable of infinite variations and this sampler shows six different ways of using it, finishing with the berry knot which combines both flat knots and cording.

Pin a short holding cord to the board. Cut eight 240 cm (8 ft) lengths of string, double them and set them on to the holding cord with lark's head knots.

Using the last thread as leader, work a row of horizontal cording.

The flat knot
This is normally made with four threads. The two centre ones are the core threads, and the two outer ones are the knotting threads. Keep the core threads taut, and work one half knot to the right.

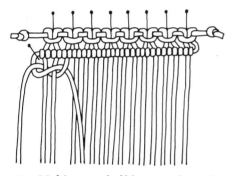

26a Making one half knot to the right

Push this knot up to the cording, then work one half knot to the left. These two half knots make one flat knot.

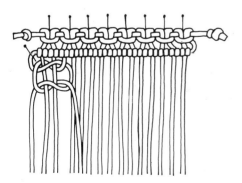

26b Making one half knot to the left, resulting in one flat knot

Make another flat knot. Depending which half knot is worked first, flat knots can be made to the right or to the left. A half knot to the right followed by one to the left, as you have just done, results in a flat knot like the one in figure 27a. A half knot to the left followed by one to the right looks like the flat knot in figure 27b.

In a sinnet of flat knots the loop lies alternately to the left and to the right. As it is sometimes difficult to remember which half knot comes next, remember that the thread coming out from *under* the loop is the next one *over* the core threads.

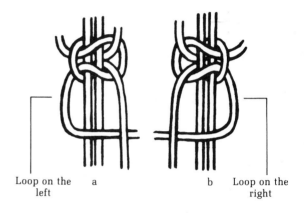

Loop on the left   a   b   Loop on the right

27 Flat knots

Make another flat knot in this group, completing a sinnet of three flat knots.

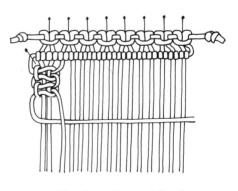

28 The first sinnet of flat knots

The loop is on the left, so the next thread to go over the core threads is the first one.

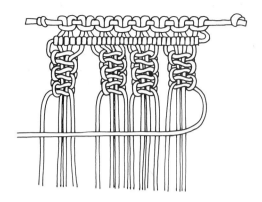

29 Four sinnets of flat knots

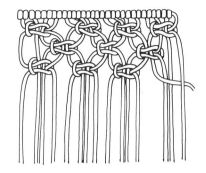

30b Alternate flat knot pattern, third row

Divide the other threads into groups of four, and work three flat knots on each. Notice that in the last knot, the loop is on the right so the next half knot is to the left. Using the first thread as leader, work one row of horizontal cording.

Alternate flat knots
This is one of the most useful knot patterns for making a fabric instead of a row of sinnets. Although this pattern is just for single alternate knots, they can be made double or treble, or one row of double and one row of single, or any combination that produces an attractive pattern.

Divide the threads into groups of four, and work one flat knot on each. Leave the first and last two threads on one side, figure 30a. Re-divide the threads into groups of four, and work one flat knot on each group. Work three rows like this, figure 30b.

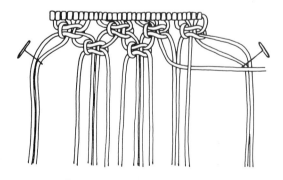

30a Alternate flat knot pattern, second row

Using the last thread as leader, work one row of horizontal cording.

Flat knot sinnet with bead
Divide the threads into groups of four. In each group make one flat knot, pass the two core threads through a bead, and work another flat knot. Use beads intended for macramé work, as those intended for jewellery do not usually have a large enough hole.

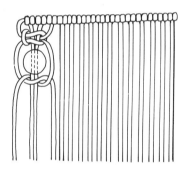

31 Flat knot sinnet with bead

Using first thread as leader, work one row of horizontal cording.

Flat knot sinnet with picots
In this section there is a flat knot sinnet with picots on either side of a multiple flat knot.

Make a flat knot with the first four threads, then make another flat knot about 5 mm (¼ in.) below. Push this knot up to the previous one, and two little loops will appear at the sides. These are picots. The size of the loops can be varied according to the distance between the flat knots.

Make a sinnet of six flat knots with picots with the first and the last four threads.

Multiple flat knot

Flat knots can be made with, and over, any reasonable number of threads. Use the centre four threads as core threads and hold them taut, and make a flat knot over them with a pair of threads from each side. Adjust length of multiple knot to match length of the sinnets each side.

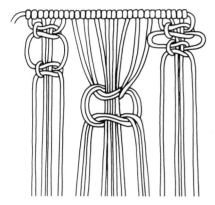

32 Flat knot sinnet with picots, centred with a multiple flat knot

Using the last thread as leader, work a row of horizontal cording.

Flat knot balls

It is possible to make flat knot sinnets three-dimensional. Divide the threads into groups of four, and on each group proceed as follows:—

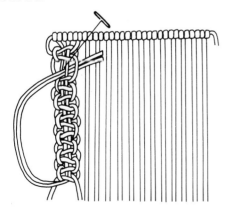

33a Flat knot ball, stage 1

Work seven flat knots. Pass the core threads from front to back through the middle of the sinnet just below the first flat knot (this can be done with a T-pin or a crochet hook), figure 33a. Pull the core threads down back into position so that the sinnet curls into a ball.

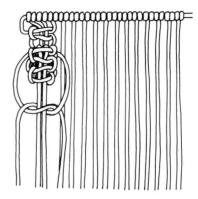

33b Flat knot ball, stage 2

Make another flat knot just below each ball to hold it in place, figure 33b. Using the first threads as leader, work a row of horizontal cording.

The berry knot

This is another three-dimensional knot. It is formed with four rows of cording bounded by flat knots on four sides, and is worked with eight threads.

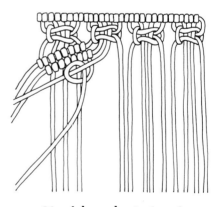

34a A berry knot, stage 1

Divide the threads into groups of four and make one flat knot on each group. Cord all the threads of the second group diagonally to the left over all four threads of the first group. Repeat with the next group of eight threads.

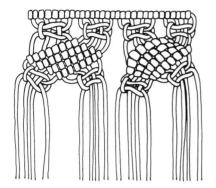

34b Berry knots, stage 2

Make a flat knot on each group of four threads.

You will notice that in figure 34b the first berry knot looks rather flat, whereas the second appears convex. To achieve this effect make the lower flat knots firm, so that they pull the cording together, and put a finger behind the cording and push it towards you, so that it makes a rounded shape like a little berry.

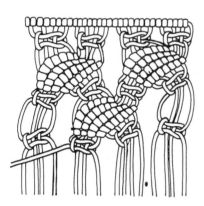

34c Alternate berry knots

Leave first four and last four threads aside, and make a berry knot over groups of eight threads in between. (In this case, only one group.)

To finish Work a row of horizontal cording. Cut the ends 5 cm (2 in.) below, and fray out to make a fringe.

Making a flat knot in one operation
It is worth learning to make a flat knot in one operation instead of making two half knots. This saves half the time spent working a pattern of flat knots.

Figures 35a to f demonstrate the method. When the two sides of the knot are pulled apart, as in figure 35e, the knot may not appear to look like figure 35f. If you pull the two loops indicated by the upper arrows first, then this section will resolve itself into the first half of the flat knot. Pull the ends indicated by the lower arrows next, and this movement will complete the flat knot with the other half knot.

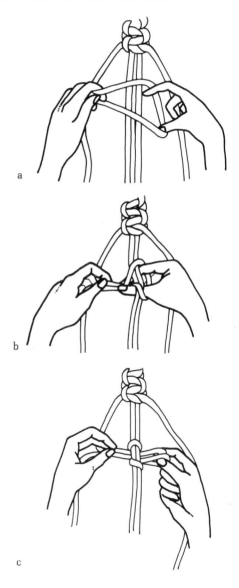

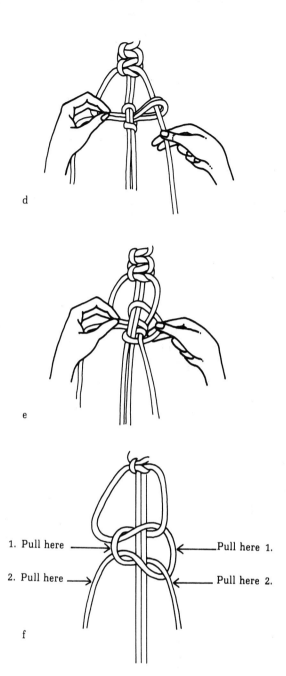

d

e

1. Pull here   →   ←   Pull here 1.

2. Pull here   →   ←   Pull here 2.

f

35a-f Making a flat knot in one operation

Sampler 4 CAVANDOLI WORK

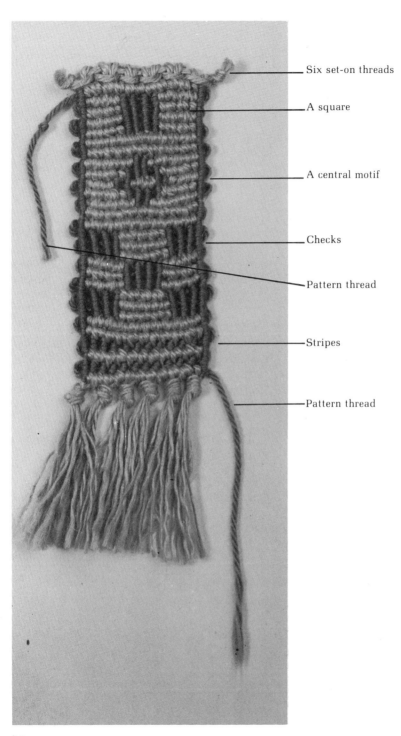

Six set-on threads

A square

A central motif

Checks

Pattern thread

Stripes

Pattern thread

This type of close cording is named after Madame Valentina Cavandoli, who developed this form of knotting in Italy at the turn of the century.

The main characteristics of the work are the tightly knotted texture, the geometric design, and the coloured picot edging. You will notice the sampler uses the same length of yarn as the others, but works up into a much shorter piece — cavandoli work uses up more yarn than ordinary knotting. It also takes longer to work.

Patterns for cavandoli are worked out on graph paper. Each square represents a knot. The blank squares are the horizontal double half hitches (ie the ordinary cording) and the crosses represent the vertical double half hitches in the contrasting colour. Only two colours are used in cavandoli work. All the set-on threads are in the background colour, and the other colour is used as leader for the horizontal cording but only appears in the pattern and on the picot edges. Set on six doubled 120 cm (4 ft) lengths to a holding cord. The pattern to be worked is the one in the graph in figure 36. The coloured pattern thread is a 300 cm (10 ft) length of *Anchor Soft Cotton* in a contrasting colour — or use a thread which is the same gauge as your string.

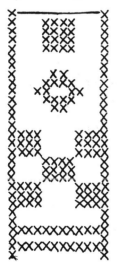

36 Graph for the cavandoli sampler

The 300 cm (10 ft) length of coloured thread will be known as the 'pattern' thread from now on.

Keep your fingers close to the knots, pull them tightly, and try not to leave gaps between the rows of horizontal cording.

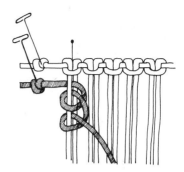

37 Starting the pattern thread, making vertical half hitches

Make an overhand knot at one end of the coloured pattern thread, and pin it to the left of the work. Wind up the rest of the thread into a figure-of-eight bundle, starting nearest the work, and secure it with a rubber band. Lengths can be drawn out as required.

Pass the pattern thread *under* the first thread, and make a vertical half hitch round the first hanging thread. Push this up to the heading, and then make another vertical half hitch on the same thread. This knot is worked in two steps, like all double half hitches, though it is shown as one movement in the diagram. When the knot is complete, test that it is correct — the pattern thread should come out between the two loops, and the knot should move easily up and down the vertical thread.

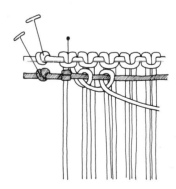

38 Working horizontal cording with pattern thread as leader

The pattern thread now becomes the leader. Work a row of horizontal cording across the next ten threads.

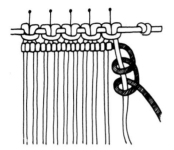

39 Making vertical half hitches on the last thread

Make two vertical half hitches on the last thread with the pattern thread, in the same way as you did on the first thread. Note that the pattern thread goes *under* the last thread before starting the knot, and that the loops go clockwise.

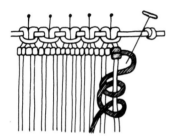

40 Making a picot on the right side

Stick a T-pin to the right of the last thread. Turn the pattern thread round the pin, pass it *under* the last thread, and work a vertical double half hitch. Note that when working from left to right the half hitch was looped clockwise, but now when working from

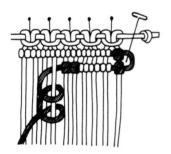

41 Working vertical half hitches going from right to left

right to left it is looped anti-clockwise. Whichever way you are working, the pattern thread always starts *under* the hanging thread.

Using the pattern thread as a leader, cord across the next three threads. Now look at the graph of the sampler. There are four crosses marked; this means that the next four threads have double half hitches worked on them vertically with the pattern thread.

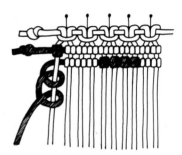

42 Making a vertical double half hitch on the last thread of the second row

Having worked the four vertical double half hitches, the pattern thread reverts to the role of leader and cords across the next three threads. When you reach the last thread, make a double vertical half hitch on it.

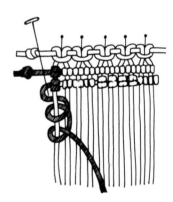

43 Making a picot on the left side

Stick a T-pin in beside the last knot, turn the pattern thread round it, pass it *under* the first thread again, then work two vertical half hitches (this time looping them clockwise).

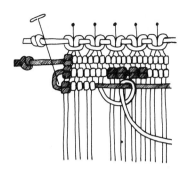

44 Using the pattern thread as leader again

Using the pattern thread as leader, cord across the next 3 threads.

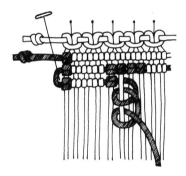

45 Working vertical half hitches going from left to right

Complete the sampler by following the graph. You are now working the second row of the block of crosses at the top. Each cross represents a vertical double half hitch made with the pattern thread, and the blank squares represent horizontal double half hitches. Below the square pattern there is an open square, a check pattern, and a couple of stripes.

Finish off by working a last plain row of horizontal cording (still with coloured edge and picot), and knot off the threads in pairs with overhand knots. Cut the ends 4 cm (1½ in.) below the knots. Fray out to make a fringe.

Part 2

THE PATTERNS

PLANT HANGERS

A simple plant hanger in thick yarn is one of the quickest and easiest things to make in macramé — though there is plenty of scope for more elaborate designs as you get more ambitious.

Plant pots are not the only objects that can be hung up in sinnets — what about goldfish bowls, or fern cases, or chair seats or table tops?

Yarn Plant hangers look best in thick yarns. A thin yarn can always be doubled or trebled. If the planter is to be kept hanging in the open, use a man made fibre, as natural fibres rot and fade. If possible, use metal rings for hanging, and check that they have a good solid join.

Lengths Planters consist mostly of sinnets, and these will need long knotting threads and rather shorter core threads. Knotting up a sample sinnet will give you an idea of the amount required for the desired length. A plant hanger with three sinnets will need three core threads and three knotting threads, making six of each when doubled.

Method Most planters are worked from the top. A strong hook in a beam in the garage, or a butchers' hook suspended from a rope wrapped round a steel beam, makes a good point from which to work. Alternatively in the house you could drive a large nail into the unseen woodwork above a doorway and work from that.

Starting There are two usual methods for starting off a planter:

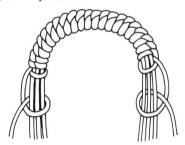

46 Buttonhole loop

Method 1 — Pass all the lengths through a ring, adjust them until they are doubled, and work from there.

Method 2 — Make a *buttonhole loop* as follows:

Cut the required number of lengths.

Centre them.

Cut a 2 m (2 yd) length and work half hitches (buttonholing) over the centre 15 cm (6 in.) of the grouped threads.

Fold the worked length to form a loop.

Cut a 1 m (1 yd) length and use it to make a wrapping over all the threads.

Finishing Most planters are finished with a large overhand knot over all threads, or a wrapping, or Chinese crown knots, finishing in a tassel. See figures 47 and 48 for instructions on these methods.

PLANT HANGER IN THICK YARN

(See also colour plate 1 facing page 72)

Measurements
Length of knotting without bowl 1.5 m (5 ft)
Bowl 25 cm (10 in.) diameter at top, 10 cm (4 in.) at bottom

Materials
48 m (52 yd) of Maxicord 5 mm (³/₁₆ in.) wide yarn
Three rings 10 cm (4 in.) diameter

Cut
Four 5 m (5½ yd) lengths
Four 7 m (7½ yd) lengths

Set-on by passing all the threads through one of the rings, and adjusting them until they all hang doubled.

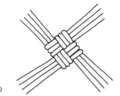

a 2 b

47a Divide the cords into four equal groups
Fold 1 over centre into West, keeping your thumb in the fold
Fold 2 over 1 into North
Fold 3 over 2 into East
Fold 4 over 3 into South through the loop over the thumb

47b Pull each end and each group separately to compose the knot, which will look like this

47 Chinese crown knot

The pattern

1 Grip the ring between the knees, divide the threads into groups of four, each group consisting of two long and two short ends, and work six Chinese crown knots.

2 Pass all the ends through another ring, make a double half hitch on to the ring with each thread in turn, keeping each group in the order one long, two short, one long.

3 In the same groups, work long sinnets as follows:
6 half knots.
*Drop down 4 cm (1½ in.) and work 1 flat knot.
Drop down another 4 cm (1½ in.), work 6 half knots.*
Work to * to * twice more.

4 Drop down 10 cm (4 in.), re-devide the groups by taking pairs from adjacent groups, and work six half knots on each group.

Repeat step 2

5 Divide threads into four groups, and work eight Chinese crown knots.

To finish Drop down about 35 cm (14 in.), cut the ends, and fray them out to make a tassel.

WALL HANGING PLANTER

Measurements
120 cm (4 ft) high.
Width about 23 cm (9 in.)
It will hold a 10 cm (4 in.) diameter pot

Materials
78 m (84 yd) of *Maxicord* — 10 mm (⅜ in.)
wide yarn
One stick 38-41 cm (15-16 in.) long
One wood ring 7.5 cm (3 in.) diameter
One wood ring 15 cm (6 in.) diameter

Cut for the hanging
Eight 5.5 m (6 yd) lengths for the hanging
Eight 2 m (2 yd) lengths to add to the ring
One 1 m (1 yd) length for wrapping the bottom

Set-on the eight 5.5 m (6 yd) lengths to the
stick, doubled, with lark's head knots.

1 Divide the threads into groups of four,
and work one flat knot on each group. Work
one alternate flat knot between the first
and the last two groups of four. Work one
flat knot on the first and last four threads.

2 Make a diamond on two rows of diagonal
cording, using the four centre threads to
knot the small ring into the middle as
shown in figure 81. At the bottom of the
diamond, cross the leaders on the right
over the ones on the left.

3 Make five rows of alternate flat knots
with the first and last eight threads. Complete the cross in double diagonal cording.

4 Incorporate the large ring as follows:
make double half hitches on to it with all

the threads in turn. Double the eight 2 m
(2 yd) lengths, and set them on the ring with
double half hitches.

5 Use the first and last threads of the
hanging as leader, and cord them round to
the front of the ring. Cross them, and continue cording diagonally over ten threads in
each direction, and then horizontally across
the rest of the threads until the leaders meet
at the back. Use the two centre threads to
make a double row of cording in front.

6 Use a 1 m (1 yd) length to make a wrapping over all threads (figures 48a and b).
Trim the ends about 30 cm (1 ft) below.

To make the hanging loop

Cut
Two 5.5 m (6 yd) lengths
Two 2 m (2 yd) lengths
One 150 cm (5 ft) length
One 1 m (1 yd) length

1 Centre the four longest threads, work
button-holing across the middle of the
group with the 150 cm (5 ft) length, fold
the grouped threads over and make a
wrapping with the 1 m (1 yd) length, as
shown in figures 48a and b.

2 Using the short lengths as core threads,
and the longer ones as knotting threads,
work sinnets of flat knots 20 cm (8 in.) long.

3 Set one sinnet on to the stick on each side
of the hanging, with double half hitches.

4 Work a short sinnet of half knots that
spirals once, and cut the ends about 15 cm
(6 in.) below. Fray out the ends to make a
tassel.

48a Cut a length of cord.
Make a loop at one end and
lay it along the bunched
cords that are to be
wrapped. Pass the long end
of the cord round the group
in tight turns, working
upwards

48b Pass the end of the cord
through the loop at the top.
Pull the bottom end until the
loop is tucked inside the
wrapping. Trim both ends so
that they are invisible.

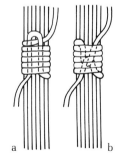

48 Making a wrapping

RIGID HANGING PLANT CONTAINER

This design is derived from the painted wire hanging baskets of the early twentieth century. It is made of polypropylene parcel twine and worked over PVC-covered lampshade rings, so that it can hang in the open for some years without rotting, and can be washed if necessary.

Measurements
Height about 1 m (1 yd)
Basket about 18 cm (7 in.) diameter

Materials
156 m (170 yd) of thick white polypropylene parcel twine
PVC-covered lampshade rings:
    One 22 cm (9 in.) diameter
    Three 15 cm (6 in.) diameter
    One 10 cm (4 in.) diameter

Cut
Forty-eight 320 cm (3½ yd) lengths

Set-on all the lengths to the largest ring as follows:

Two lengths at a time. Fold them so that one end is 30 cm (1 ft) longer than the other, and set them on with double half hitches and simple picots, so that the two shorter threads hang in the middle of each group of four, as shown in figure 49.

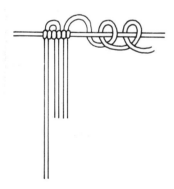

49 Setting on with double half hitches and simple picots

The pattern

1 On each group of four, work a sinnet of ten flat knots.

2 Pass all the ends through a 15 cm (6 in.) ring, make a double half hitch on to the ring with each knotting thread in turn, leaving the core threads idle.

3 Work six rows of alternate flat knots

Repeat step 2

4 Divide the threads into groups of eight. In each group work a diamond in cording, with a central flat knot, crossing neighbouring leaders half-way through the diamond.

5 Pass all ends through a 15 cm (6 in.) ring. Cord groups of four on to the ring as follows: cord first thread on to the ring with a double half hitch. Loop the next two threads over the ring with a single half hitch and hold them taut. Cord the last thread on to the ring with a double half hitch. With these four threads make a sinnet of eight flat knots.

6 Cut off core threads. Pass remaining knotting threads through the 10 cm (4 in.) ring, and make double half hitches on to it with each thread in turn.

7 Using a 1 m (1 yd) length, make a wrapping over all thread.

8 Divide the threads into four equal groups, and work one Chinese crown knot. Using the two longest threads in each group as knotting threads, work five flat knots.

9 Gather all the ends together and with a 1 m (1 yd) length make a wrapping. Cut the ends about 18 cm (7 in.) below the wrapping.

Hanging chains

Cut
Three 360 cm (4 yd) lengths

Pass each length through the top 15 cm (6 in.) ring at an equal distance apart. Work single knotted chain for 45 cm (18 in.). Join all three sinnets together with an overhand knot. Divide the threads into two groups, use the longest thread in each group to work ten vertical half hitches over the others. Make another overhand knot over all the threads. Tighten the knot, trim the ends.

HANGING CARBOY

Measurements
Approximately 150 cm (5 ft) high

Materials
106 m (115 yd) of 5 mm (³/₁₆ in.) wide
Homespun Jute
1 carboy about 38 cm (15 in.) high
1 glass float, about 15 cm (6 in.) high
1 wooden ring, about 15 cm (6 in.) diameter

Cut
Eight 900 cm (10 yd) lengths
Eight 360 cm (4 yd) lengths
One 180 cm (2 yd) length for buttonholing
One 90 cm (1 yd) length for a wrapping

1 Centre the eight longest threads. Use the 180 cm (2 yd) length to work about 18 cm (7 in.) of vertical half hitches (button-holing) in the centre of the grouped threads. Double the whole length over, and make a wrapping with the 90 cm (1 yd) length.

2 Grip the loop between the knees, divide the cords into four equal groups and work 9 Chinese crown knots.

3 In the same groups, work sinnets of flat knots long enough to fit round the float. Arrange the sinnets evenly round, tie all the ends together underneath, and secure the back of each sinnet to the glass with clear glue. Leave to dry before continuing the work.

4 Divide the cords into four equal groups, and work 7 Chinese crown knots. After the first,

undo the tie, and pull the knot into position close to the float.

In the same groups but exchanging core threads and knotting threads, work half knot sinnets about 7.5 cm (3 in.) long. Set these on to the ring at equal distances with double half hitches (figure 50). Continue with flat knot sinnets about 13 cm (5 in.) long.

6 Using an attached leader, cord the hanging threads round the neck of the bottle, setting on two double 360 cm (4 yd) lengths in between each sinnet with double half hitches — (or, if the neck is narrow, with reversed lark's head knots). Keeping the same leader work another row of cording tightly round the neck of the bottle.

7 Divide the threads into groups of four, work sinnets of 6 flat knots.

8 Bring the sinnets together in pairs. In each group of eight threads work 12 flat knots with the two longest threads as knotting threads. (Make this more if the carboy is taller than 38 cm (15 in.).

9 Re-divide sinnets into groups of four and work 9 flat knots on each, using the longest threads as knotting threads.

10 Combine the sinnets into groups of eight again, and work enough flat knots with the longest threads to bring the sinnets together underneath the centre of the carboy.

11 Tie a spare thread tightly round all the hanging threads. Turn the carboy upside down and work a Chinese crown knot. Take off the tied thread, and adjust the Chinese knot to fit the carboy closely. Pull all the threads so that the sinnets fit snugly round the carboy. Work a few more Chinese crown knots.

To finish Trim the ends level about 30 cm (1 ft) below the last knot. Fray them out to make a tassel.

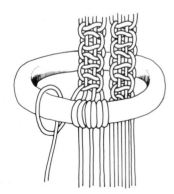

50 Cording threads on to a ring with double half hitches

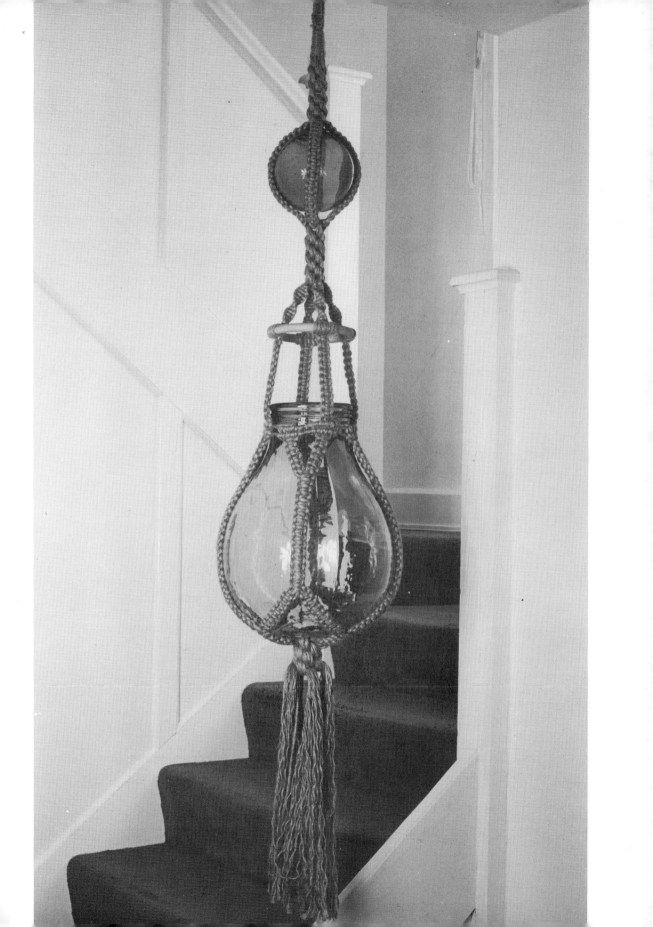

TABLE MATS

A number of patterns are given for table mats because the square, rectangular and round shapes can be adapted to many uses, and a small mat is a good way to begin.

Yarns should be washable, soft enough not to scratch a polished surface, and thick enough to form a heat-resistant pad. Many types of natural and synthetic yarns are worth trying out. Linen looks attractive and dyes and washes well, and the same goes for cotton.

Patterns need to be of uniform thickness so that articles placed on the mat do not tip over. If the same kind of knotting has to be used throughout, variety can be introduced with the use of different colours, which can enliven the pattern and define the edges.

Techniques. Mats are small enough to be worked in entirety on the knotting board. Lengths are usually the standard eight times the measurements of the knotting (four times when doubled), with the addition of a few inches for fringing, if used.

Rectangular mats with a fringe each end are simple to make and are a good way of practising a pattern. They are set on in a particular way on pins, as shown in figure 51, so that both ends will look the same.

Square mats can be worked simply as a square, or in sections in cording like the mat on page 46, or starting from the middle, like the cushion on page 66, with a fringe all round. In the latter case, the centre would have to be interlaced threads and not sinnets, which would make the surface of the mat very uneven.

Round mats are worked from a ring in the centre, which could be a curtain ring, or made of thread or wire, or maybe a rubber washer. Threads are added as the radius of the mat increases, and the outer edges can be finished in various interesting ways.

Finishing off should be particularly firm and secure for mats as they will need frequent washing. Fringes are a good finish, but check first that the chosen yarn is still strong when unravelled; some yarns shred away in the wash. Edges can be bound with tape, turned under and sewn into the back, secured with machine stitching, or finished with tight overhand knots painted over with glue that will survive washing.

RECTANGULAR MAT IN TWO COLOURS IN A DIAGONAL CORDING PATTERN

Measurements
28 cm x 44 cm (11 in. x 17 in.)

Materials
2 mm (¹/₁₆ in.) soft cotton in two colours
74 m (80 yd) of a light colour
17 m (18 yd) of a dark colour

Cut
Light colour — Twenty four 300 cm (10 ft) lengths
Dark colour — Five 180 cm (6 ft) lengths; two 360 cm (12 ft) lengths

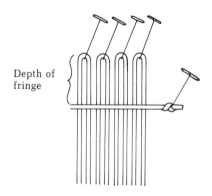

Depth of fringe

51 Setting threads on for a fringe, looped over pins

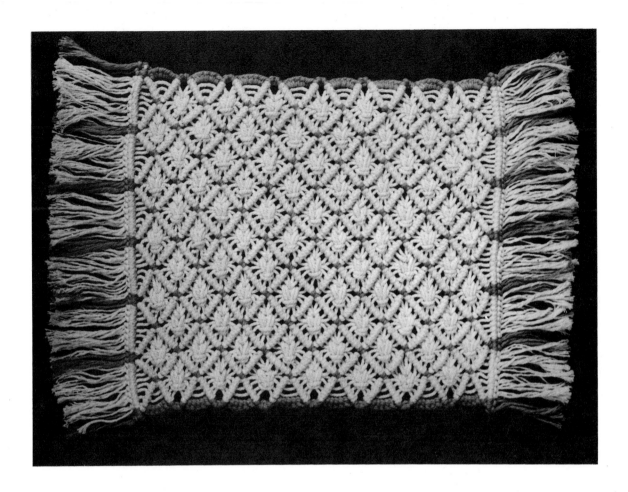

Set-on Hang doubled threads on pins as shown in figure 51. Using the twenty-four light 300 cm (10 ft) lengths, and the five dark 180 cm (6 ft) lengths, hang them in the following order:

(4 light 1 dark) five times, 4 light.

At each end hang the 360 cm (12 ft) dark lengths, folded 270 cm (9 ft) and 90 cm (3 ft); 90 cm (3 ft) and 270 cm (9 ft) with the longest threads on the outside.

With the dark attached leader work a row of horizontal cording across all threads 10 cm (4 in.) below the pins.

The pattern
1 Work three vertical half hitches with the longer dark thread over the shorter at each end of the row.

2 Cord the pairs of dark threads in between diagonally to left and right (L and R) — first the R leader to the right over four light threads, then the L leader to the left over four light threads and one dark thread.

3 Make a flat knot with each group of eight light threads, with a pair of knotting threads each side over four core threads.

4 At the sides, turn the dark leaders and cord them back towards the centre over two dark and four light threads.

5 Complete the diamond shapes by cording all the dark leaders diagonally as in step 2, and continue in pattern for about 30 cm (12 in.), making six vertical half hitches with the longer dark thread at each side over the shorter one in between each diamond

pattern. Finish with a row of horizontal cording with an attached dark thread.

6 Make an overhand knot over each thread close to the cording, cut ends about 5 cm (2 in.) below the knotting, fray out to make a fringe.

7 At the beginning, cut the loops, then repeat step 6.

To finish Sew in the ends of the attached leaders.

RECTANGULAR TABLE MAT IN TWO COLOURS IN A FLAT KNOT PATTERN

Measurements
48 cm x 24 cm (19 in. x 9½ in.) including fringe

Materials
Soft cotton 2 mm (¹/₁₆ in.) wide in two colours
52 m (56 yd) of a light colour
47 m (51 yd) of a dark colour

Cut
Fourteen light-coloured 360 cm (4 yd) lengths
Thirteen dark-coloured 315 cm (3½ yd) lengths
Two dark-coloured 200 cm (2¼ yd) lengths for each end
Two dark-coloured 45 cm (½ yd) lengths for attached leaders.

Set-on as follows:
Make an overhand knot at the end of a single dark 200 cm (2¼ yd) thread and pin it to the board.

Hang a row of doubled threads from pins at the same level, alternatively light and dark across the row, ending with another single dark thread hanging from a knot.

Use a dark attached leader to cord across all threads at least 10 cm (4 in.) below the pins, as in figure 51.

The pattern
1 Work seven rows of alternate flat knots.

2 Leave aside the first two and last two threads. Divide remaining threads into

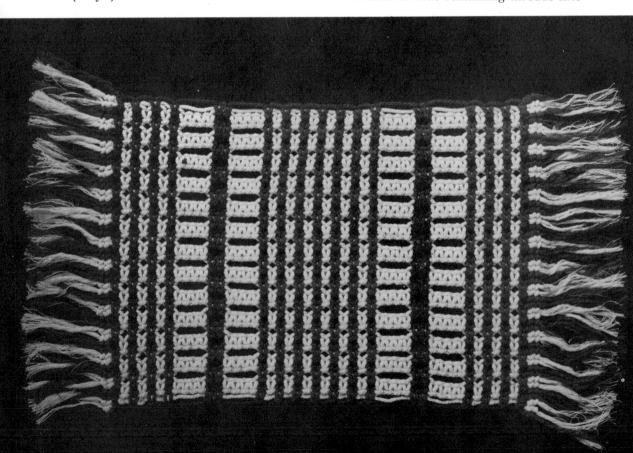

groups of four, work 4 flat knots in each group (light coloured sinnets).

3 Using all the threads again, divide them into groups of four and work 2 flat knots on each group (dark coloured sinnets).

Repeat step 2.

4 Using all the threads work thirteen rows of alternate flat knots. (Note: do not pull the knots too tightly, keep them pinned in place and keep the edges straight, otherwise this section of the mat may have a 'waist' in the middle).

Repeat step 2, step 3, step 2 and step 1.

5 Using attached dark 45 cm (½ yd) leader, work one row of cording across all threads. *Make an overhand knot over each thread close to the cording. Trim the ends 6 cm (2½ in.) below knots, as shown for a fringe on page 84. Fray out the ends. Sew in the ends of the attached leader.

6 At the beginning, cut the loops and work from * to * of step 5.

RECTANGULAR TABLE MAT IN THREE COLOURS IN A FLAT KNOT PATTERN

Measurements
23 cm x 38 cm (9 in. x 15 in.)

Materials
Country Jute 3 mm (⅛ in.) wide
Tan 37 m (40 yd)
Black 23 m (25 yd)
Cream 23 m (25 yd)

Cut
In tan — six 255 cm (8½ ft) lengths; six 300 cm (10 ft) lengths; four 30 cm (1 ft) lengths.
In black — four 255 cm (8½ ft) lengths; four 300 cm (10 ft) lengths
In cream — four 255 cm (8½ ft) lengths; four 300 cm (10 ft) lengths

Set-on by hanging the doubled threads on pins, as in figure 51 and working the first row of cording across 7.5 cm (3 in.) below the pins (step 1).

Each colour group consists of four doubled threads, the outer ones 300 cm (10 ft) long, the two inner ones 255 cm (8½ ft) long. Set them on in colour groups in the following order: tan, cream, black, tan, cream, black, tan.

The pattern
1 With attached tan leader, cord across all threads.

2 In each colour group of eight threads work a flat knot, with a pair of threads each side over four core threads.

Repeat step 1.

3 Work in alternate flat knots for nine rows.

Repeat step 2, step 3, step 2, step 3, step 1, step 2 and lastly step 1 again.

Finish off by trimming the ends 4 cm (1½ in.) below the last row of cording, fray them out to make a fringe.

At the beginning, cut the loops, trim the length to match the other end, and fray out.

SQUARE CORDED MAT

Measurements
Approximately 15 cm (6 in.) square

Materials
26 m (28 yd) of *Homespun Jute* 5 m (³/₁₆ in.) wide.

Note To keep this mat square and neat, mark a 15 cm (6 in.) square on the board, and pin the work firmly in line with it.

Cut A holding cord 1 m (1 yd) long
Sixteen 150 cm (5 ft) lengths

Set-on as follows:
Use the short length as a holding cord, measure 20 cm (8 in.) from one end and make an overhand knot. Pin the knot to the top right corner of the square marked on the board. The length to the left (the longest) is the horizontal holding cord across the top of the square. Set

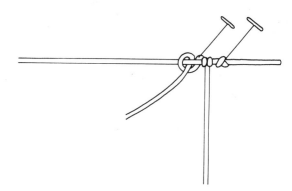

52 Setting threads on with double half hitches

on eight doubled threads with double half hitches (figure 52). At this point let the end of the holding cord hang down vertically, and set on two more doubled threads, which will lie horizontally (figure 53a).

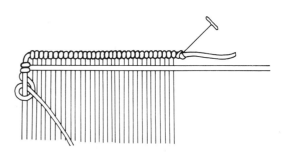

53a Setting on to a vertical holding cord

The pattern
Cord the four threads on the vertical holding cord horizontally to the right in turn, across the first four hanging threads. Cord the next four hanging threads vertically in turn from top to bottom across the four rows of horizontal cording as shown in figure 53b. Repeat from * to * once.

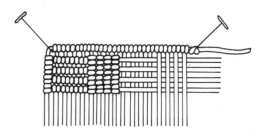

53b Making a square corded pattern

Set two more doubled threads (with doubled half hitches) on to the vertical holding cord, and repeat from * to * across the row.

Repeat until all eight threads are set on the vertical holding cord, and worked across.

To finish Undo the knot in the top right corner, and cord the rest of the holding cord down the right side of the mat, from top to bottom.

Cord the other end of the holding cord across the bottom of the mat, over all threads, including the other end of the holding cord.

Trim all the ends to about 2 cm (¾ in.). Turn them under, and glue or sew them to the back of the mat.

ROUND CAVANDOLI MAT

Measurements
Approximately 20 cm (8 in.) diameter

Materials
Country Jute 3 mm (⅛ in.) wide
77 m (84 yd) of the background colour
4 m (4 yd) of a lighter colour
2 m (2 yd) of a darker colour

The light thread is used as the 'pattern thread' as in cavandoli work — that is to say, it is used alternately as a leader for the cording, and as a knotting thread for the vertical half hitches forming the coloured pattern. Two-thirds of the way through the mat, the light pattern thread is replaced by the darker one.

Cut the background threads in four diminishing lengths, and use the longest ones first.

Twenty 120 cm (4 ft) lengths
Twenty 105 cm (3½ ft) lengths
Twenty 90 cm (3 ft) lengths
Twenty 60 cm (2 ft) lengths

(It may be necessary to cut more)

Set-on as follows:
Make a knot at one end of the light thread, set six threads on next to the knot, doubled, with lark's head knots, pin the knot to the centre of the board and curl the set-on threads round it in a tight circle.

The pattern
Work a row of cording round the circle using the light holding cord as leader, setting on one thread of the background colour in between each pair of hanging threads.

Work another circuit in the same way.

On the third circuit use the light thread to make single vertical half hitches over two threads, double vertical half hitches over the next three, and single vertical half hitches over the last two.

Use the light thread as leader to work three more rows of cording all round.

After the first few rows, it will be found that adding a new thread in between each pair of hanging threads is too much. From now on add threads only as required, when there is a gap in the cording.

In the next row make vertical half hitches over 28 threads, first single, then double, then single again. In the following row make vertical half hitches under the central 12 threads only of this group.

Work another five rows of cording, then exchange the light thread for the darker one (sew the ends into the back of the mat afterwards). Make another vertical half hitch pattern over about 15 threads, in the position shown in the photograph.

Cord two more rows round the mat, then make a vertical half hitch pattern over about 60 threads.

Continue cording round the mat until it is of the desired size.

To finish The edge can either be left plain, or worked in the irregular fashion shown in the photograph. To make an irregular edge, proceed as follows:

Leave dark leader idle.

Use one of the hanging threads to cord round the mat over four to six hanging threads. Go back one or two threads and use it to cord round over the next four to six threads.

Work in this way all round the mat.

Cut the ends about 12 mm (½ in.) away from the last row of cording, turn them under, and sew or glue them on to the back of the mat.

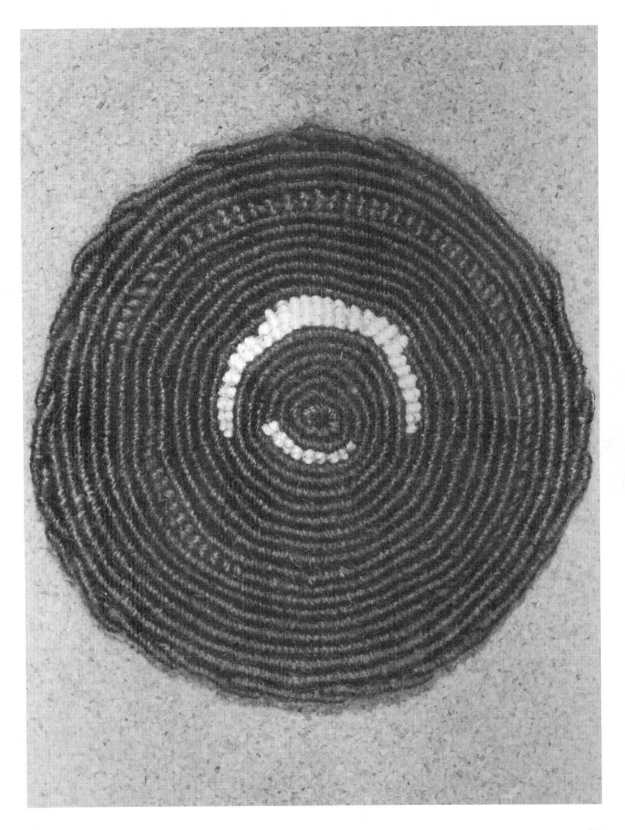

ROUND MAT IN FINE KNOTTING

Measurements
25 cm (10 in.) diameter, including fringe

Materials
82 m (90 yd) of *Twilley's No 2 health vest cotton*
One 2.5 cm (1 in.) ring

Cut
Twenty 120 cm (4 ft) lengths (step 1)
Ten 105 cm (3½ ft) lengths (step 2)
Twenty 75 cm (2½ ft) lengths (repeat of step 2)
Fifty 60 cm (2 ft) lengths (step 5)
Odd lengths for attached leaders

Set-on Double the twenty 120 cm (4 ft) lengths and set them on to the ring with lark's head knots.

The pattern

1 Work two rows of alternate flat knots. On the third row make sinnets of 3 flat knots.

2 Work a row of horizontal cording all round, using an attached leader. Set one doubled thread on to the leader in between each sinnet, using double half hitches.

3 Divide the threads into groups of three and work 5 half knots on each group, making a half knot sinnet that spirals once. Pin each sinnet in place as it is worked.

Repeat step 2.

4 Work seven rows of alternate flat knots. Work from the centre outwards, turning the board as necessary, and increasing the distance between the rows and the knots as the work gets further from the centre.

5 Work a row of horizontal cording all round, using an attached leader. Set two doubled threads on to the leader in between each sinnet, using double half hitches (see figure 52).

Repeat step 3 (the last sinnet will have four threads, not three).

6 Work a row of cording all round, using an attached leader.

7 Divide the threads into groups of twelve. In each group work as follows:

Make 2 flat knots with the centre 4 threads.
Make 1 flat knot with the group of 3 threads on each side.
Cord the first thread into the centre over 5 threads.
Cord the last thread into the centre over 6 threads.
Make an overhand knot over the 2 centre threads.

To finish Trim the ends to about 2.5 cm (1 in.) from the overhand knot. Fray the yarn out to make a fringe. Sew in the ends of the attached leaders.

JEWELLERY

Ideas for jewellery often derive from a happy conjunction of yarns, beads and fabrics, and a small pretty accessory can often add the finishing touch to an outfit. For example, a grey silk shirt with a tan velvet skirt may be linked with a gold and grey belt, or dressed up with a silver collar with tan beads and crystal drops. A cavandoli choker can be used to pick out a pattern in a print. An armful of silk bracelets can complement a subtle colour scheme. In a more informal way, a shell can be hung on a macramé cord for summer or beach wear, or polished stones can be suspended in leather thonging to go with winter sweaters.

Yarns For such bit and pieces almost anything can be used that will hold a knot. However, the materials used for the patterns that follow all require different treatment and achieve different effects.

Metal thread The type used for the chain necklace opposite and the tiny strip bracelet, page 84 is a metal sewing thread called *SI*, by Schurer, which comes in a 10 m (10 yd) hank. The cavandoli watch strap, colour plate 2 facing page 73, is made of the silver, with the pattern thread in gold. Using the angling method described on page 102, tiny metallic flowers can be made up in this thread, and used as suggested in the page of sketches in that section.

Lustrecord This is marketed in the UK by Atlas Handicrafts, and consists of a rayon core wrapped with lurex. It comes in 22 m (25 yd) hanks in gold, silver and red gold. It is very good for elegant evening collars, like the ones in the photos on page 53 and 55, and small motifs can be used on evening bags or as trimmings and edgings. This yarn needs to be handled lightly, and should not be used in very long lengths. The ends should be secured with an overhand knot before work is commenced.

Leather thonging Use the fine thonging, and make sure the pieces are long enough to complete the knottings, as ends are difficult to replace. Sinnets in leather take more length than is usual. One attractive effect of working in thonging is that the loops on one side of a sinnet will consistently show the shiny side of the leather and the loops on the other will show the suede side. Sinnets are best worked with only one core thread, otherwise they are rather thick.

FINE GOLD CHAIN WITH BEADS

Measurements
About 100 cm (40 in.) long

Materials
Two hanks of *Schurer SI* metal thread in gold
5 oval beads about 20 mm (¾ in.) long
5 round 4-5 mm (⅛ in. - ³/₁₆ in.) beads
9 smaller beads

Cut a core thread double the required length of the chain.
A whole hank 10 m (10 yd) doubled for the knotting threads.

Set-on Start with an overhand knot over all four threads. At the end of the work undo this, and join all eight ends together, and make a tight overhand knot over them, cut closely, and paint clear nail varnish over the knot.

The pattern
This chain is simply a long sinnet, worked alternately in half knots and flat knots, with beads of different sizes and shapes threaded on to the core threads at intervals.

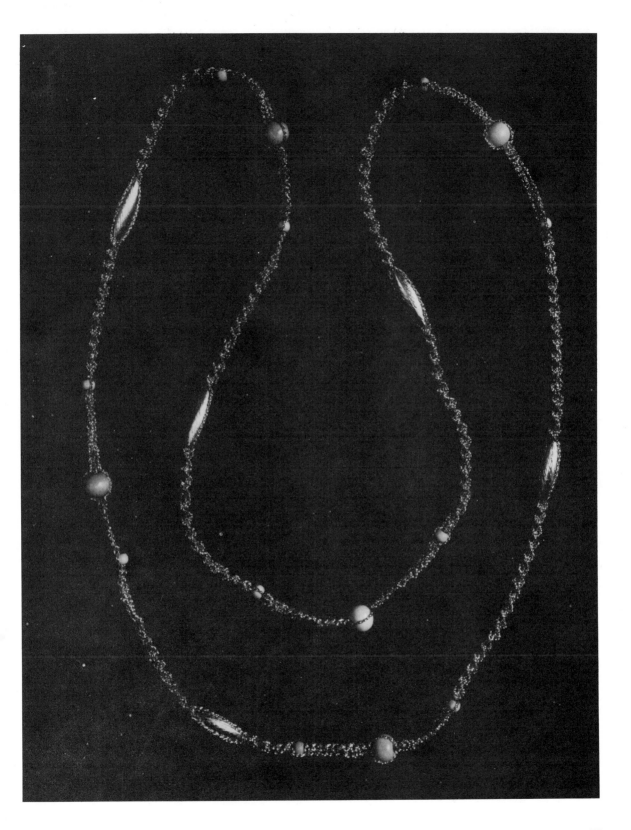

53

LUSTRECORD COLLAR WITH LARGE AND SMALL BEADS

Measurements
33 cm (13 in.) round the neck — another motif or two can be added if required
Depth 7 cm (2½ in.)

Materials
87 m (95 yd) of *Lustrecord*
Fourteen large (about 10 mm-15 mm) (⅜ in.-9/16 in.) beads
Twenty-eight small (about 5-8 mm) (³/16 in.-⅜ in.) beads
One hook and eye
Clear nail varnish

Cut
Eighty-eight 75 cm (2½ ft) lengths
Thirty 60 cm (2 ft) lengths
Two 30 cm (1 ft) lengths
One 45 cm (18 in.) length for an attached leader

Set-on in the standard way for collars as described on page 56.

To work one motif

1 Set-on doubled, to the holding cord, working from right to left, one 30 cm (1 ft) length, five 75 cm (2½ ft) lengths.

2 With attached leader, work a row of cording across all threads.

3 Make a flat knot with the first four threads on the left, pass the core threads through a small bead, and make another flat knot. Repeat with the last four threads. Make an overhand knot over the last pair of threads, cut the ends, and paint over the knot with clear varnish. (This is one end of the collar).

4 There are now four unworked threads hanging in the centre. Cord the two centre threads out over 1 thread, double two 60 cm (2 ft) lengths and set them on to these leaders with reversed lark's head knots, then with the same leader cord over two threads from each group on either side, as shown in figure 54a. Make a second row of diagonal cording with the two central threads over 5 threads each side.

5 Make a flat knot over the central two threads with a pair of threads each side, pass the core threads through a large bead and make another flat knot.

6 Cord the outside leaders back into the centre twice. Knot off the ends as shown in figure 54b.

7 Set on six more doubled 75 cm (2½ ft) lengths to the holding cord, cord across with the attached leader, and work another motif as far as step 6.

8 In between each motif, work a flat knot over the four threads, pass the core

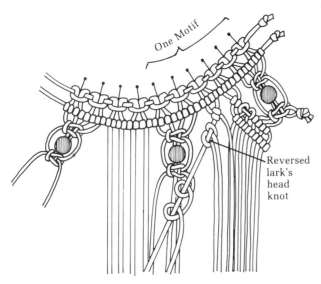

54a Starting to work the collar

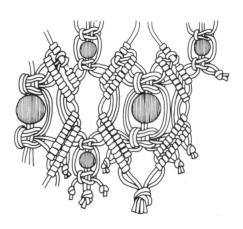

54b A completed motif

threads through a small bead, work
another flat knot, and knot off the ends,
as shown in figure 54b.

Repeat the motifs until the collar is long
enough. The very last doubled thread of the
last motif will be the 30 cm (1 ft) length,
which is knotted off to match the first one.

To finish Sew in the cords of the holding
cord and attached leader. Sew a hook to one
end of the collar and an eye to the other.
Paint over the knots with clear nail varnish.

NARROW GOLD COLLAR WITH GREEN GLASS BEADS

(see also colour plate facing page 73)

Measurements
To fit 33 cm-36 cm (13 in.-14 in.) neck size
Depth 5 cm (2 in.)

Materials
37 m (40 yd) of *Lustrecord* in gold
One hank of stranded embroidery cotton in green
33 green glass pony beads
Clear nail varnish

Cut
Sixty-six 50 cm (20 in.) lengths of *Lustrecord*
Five 45 cm (18 in.) lengths of *Lustrecord* for holding cord and attached leaders
Two 450 cm (5 yd) lengths of embroidery thread (approximate amount)

How to set up a collar on the board
Draw a circle 15 cm (6 in.) in diameter on the knotting board. Make an overhand knot at one end of a holding cord and loop this round the circle. Cut enough lengths for the first motif, double them, and set them on to the holding cord with lark's head knots. Make an overhand knot at one end of an attached leader, and pin this under the knot on the holding cord. Cord over the first group of set-on threads, and pin each lark's head knot in place round the circle as the cording is worked. From this point on patterns differ, but this is a general method for starting off collars and necklets and cuffs and other semi-circular items.

To work one motif
1 Set-on six doubled lengths of *Lustrecord*.

2 Work a row of cording with an attached leader.

3 Work a row of double vertical half hitches with the green thread, as shown in figure 55.

Repeat step 2.

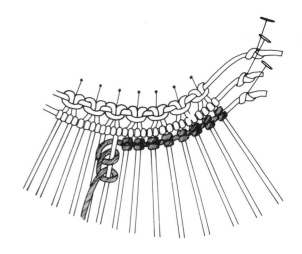

55 Working a row of vertical half hitches round a collar

4 Divide the threads into groups of four. Pass the two centre threads in each group through a bead, make a flat knot.

Repeat step 2.

Repeat step 3.

Repeat step 2, but this time work an extra half hitch over the leader every four threads to allow for the increasing radius.

5 In each group of twelve threads, work diminishing rows of alternate flat knots (3 rows). Knot off pairs of threads close to the work, pull tightly, and cut the ends close to the knot. Brush over each knot with clear nail varnish.

To finish When a sufficient number of motifs have been worked round the collar, finish off each end as follows: cord the holding cord across all threads to the outer edge. Cord the end of each attached leader in turn across a diminishing number of threads. Turn all the ends under and sew them in to the back.

Sew a hook on one end of the collar, and an eye on to the other.

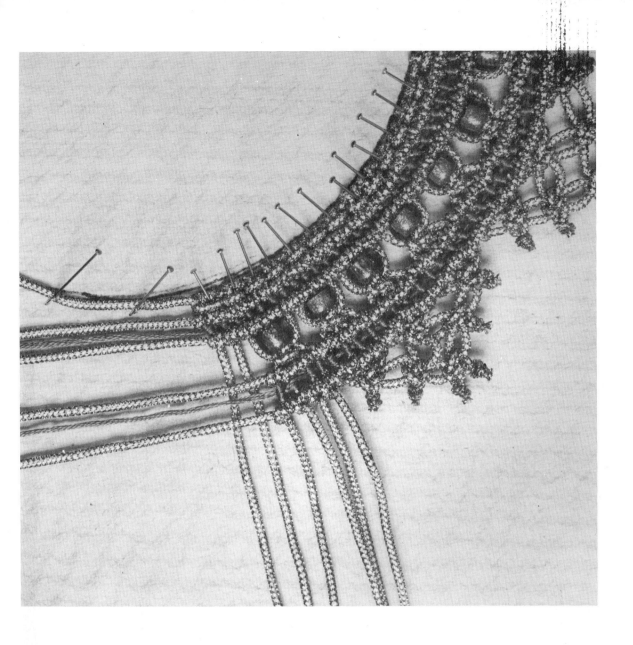

58

NECKLET IN LUSTRECORD WITH GLASS BEADS

Measurements
The circlet is 15 cm (6 in.) in diameter, and the depth at the front of the necklet is 7.5 cm (3 in.)

Materials
One metal neck circlet
38 m (41 yd) of silver *Lustrecord*
Fifty 8 mm (¼ in.) rough clear glass beads

Cut
Forty-six 30 cm (1 ft) lengths
Eight 60 cm (2 ft) lengths
Twenty 90 cm (3 ft) lengths

Set-on all threads doubled, with lark's head knots, in the following order.

1 Start at the clasp at the back, and work units of two set-on 30 cm (1 ft) threads as follows:— *Make a flat knot, pass the core threads through a bead, make another flat knot. Make an overhand knot over all four threads, and pull each separate end firmly. Cut the ends very close to the knot. Brush over the knot with clear nail varnish. This makes a polished knob rather than a knot, and adds to the decorative effect.* Repeat from * to * eleven times each side.

2 The front group of 22 doubled set-on threads are worked in rows of alternate flat knots with beads, as can clearly be seen in the photograph. As the width is reduced, the pairs of threads or groups of four threads at the sides are knotted off as described in step 1.

The arrangement of the knotting depends largely on the kind of beads you are using, and as you are unlikely to have exactly the same kind as used here, you will probably prefer to make your own pattern of them.

LEATHER NECKLACE WITH THREE HANGING STONES

(See also colour plate 3 facing page 96)

Measurements
The flat knot sinnets are each 18 cm (7 in.) long
The bottom of the longest pendant is 9 cm (3½ in.) below the centre of the sinnets

Materials
7.5 m (8 yd) of fine leather thonging.
Three polished stones

Cut
One 75 cm (2½ ft) length
Two 180 cm (6 ft) lengths
Three 90 cm (3 ft) lengths

Set-on Centre the 75 cm (2½ ft) length and the two 180 cm (6 ft) lengths on the board. Use them as a multiple holding card, and set-on the three 90 cm (3 ft) lengths, doubled, with lark's head knots.

1 Work the required number of single knotted chains on each little pendant strap — it may be that your stones are of different sizes, and the length of the strap will depend on how you wish to arrange them.

2 Glue the stones in place as shown in figure 56. Turn the stone until you find the most attractive facet. Apply clear glue thinly down the inner side of one thong. Place

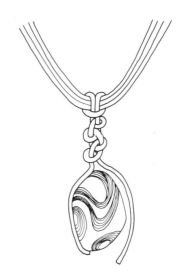

56 Method of enclosing stones in leather thonging

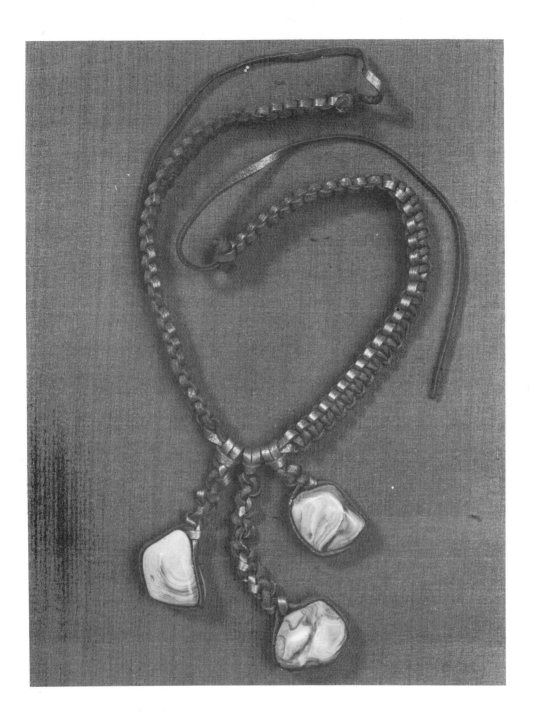

stone in position and hold thong against it. Keep up the pressure until the glue holds. If the stone is large, work on small lengths of the thonging.

Repeat with the thong on the other side. Cut off the surplus leather and press the join together with another tiny addition

of glue. The secret of enclosing stones in leather thongs is patience. Work slowly, only glue a small length at a time, leave it to dry thoroughly before handling.

3 After the three stones have been glued in place, complete the necklace by working sinnets of flat knots from the ends of the

holding cords. Leave the core thread ends to be tied at the back, and knot off the knotting threads as shown in figure 57.

57 Knotting off leather sinnets

STARS

The stars on the tree in colour plate 2 are made of *Lustrecord*. Stars can be worked in all kinds of yarn, and made in varying sizes and with different numbers of points. Lengths of yarn are set on to a ring, and each point is worked separately in a pattern of alternate flat knots with beads. The same pattern can be adapted to a collar if worked on a holding cord. Figure 58a shows a typical star pattern. The instructions below are for a smaller star using less yarn, as shown in figure 58b.

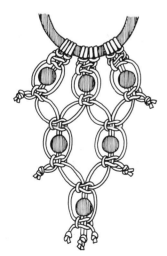

58a Alternate flat knot pattern for a large star point

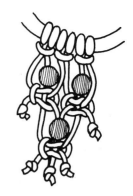

58b Alternate flat knot pattern for a small star

RED STAR

See colour plate 2 facing page 73

Measurements
7½ cm (3 in.) across the points

Materials
One 2½ cm (1 in.) diameter curtain ring
450 cm (5 yd) of *Lustrecord* in firegold
Fifteen red pony beads

Cut
Fifteen 30 cm (1 ft) lengths

Set-on doubled to the ring, with lark's head knots.

To work one point
1 Use six hanging threads, and divide them into two groups of three. In each group make a flat knot, pass the centre thread through a bead, and make another flat knot.

2 Make an overhand knot over the first thread. Cut it close to the knot and brush it over with clear nail varnish. Repeat with the last thread.

3 Make a flat knot with the remaining four threads, pass the two core threads through a bead, make another flat knot.

Repeat step 2.

4 Make an overhand knot over the last two threads, cut the ends, and brush over with clear nail varnish.

Work four more points in the same way.

61

CUSHIONS

Cushion covers are generally worked on the board, and then sewn to a fabric cover. As knotting is an openwork technique, choose a background colour which will show off the knotting design.

59 Cavandoli braid. Graph for the braid on the cushion

Yarns Soft but thick yarns are recommended for cushion covers, such as rug wool, chunky knitting wools and *Bulkycord*. Unless you are prepared to spend a lot of time, do not use anything finer than double-double knitting wool. Some rug wools are very hard, but others are soft and loosely twisted, and the man-

made ones are generally lighter in weight than pure wool. *Bulkycord* works up into a surprisingly soft fabric, but gives a strongly three-dimensional effect as can be seen in the cushions on pages 65 and 69. Other yarns can be used if there is only a small amount of knotting, such as a fringe or a braid. A tubular rayon cord fringe looks very good with velvet, and metal threads can be used for edging braids. Cavandoli strips made of crochet cottons are useful for linking the areas when cushions are made up of odd lengths of different fabrics, like the one opposite. The graph for this is shown in figure 59.

Patterns A simple pattern in one colour is often surprisingly effective, as the main impression is one of an interesting texture. However, many of the more elaborate two- and three-colour patterns are well displayed on the rounded surface of a cushion. Apart from the patterns given, any of those for table mats can easily be used for cushions if scaled up and worked in softer yarns. The design for the firescreen on page 97 looks well worked in soft double-double knitting wool, with the vertical half hitching in a darker shade, or possibly in another texture.

SQUARE CUSHION IN ALTERNATE HALF KNOT SINNETS

Measurements
14 in. (35 cm) square

Materials
104 m (113 yd) of off-white *Bulkycord*
1 cushion cover 35 cm (14 in.) square, with pad

Cut
Thirty-six 270 cm (3 yd) lengths
1 holding cord and 2 attached leaders
45 cm (18 in.) long

Set-on doubled threads to the holding cord with lark's head knots.

The pattern

1 With attached leader, work a row of horizontal cording.

2 Divide the threads into groups of four. Work 7 half knots on each group, so that each sinnet spirals once. Pin the sinnets in place as they are worked.

3 Leave the first and last two threads aside. Divide the threads into groups of four and work 7 half knots on each group. Move the pins down from the previous row as each sinnet is completed.

Continue this pattern of alternate flat knot sinnets until the work measures 35 cm (14 in.), finishing at a convenient point. It is better for the work to be slightly too long than too short. Repeat step 1.

To finish Either trim the ends, turn them under and sew them into the back, or make a decorative edge as follows:

Divide the threads into pairs, make an overhand knot over each pair close to the cording. Pull each single thread firmly to tighten the knot, and cut the ends.

To make up Sew in the ends of the holding cord and attached leaders. Lay the work on the cushion cover and pin it in place. Sew the top and bottom to the cover just within the piped edge. Secure the sides by sewing only the idle pairs in every other row to the sides of the cover.

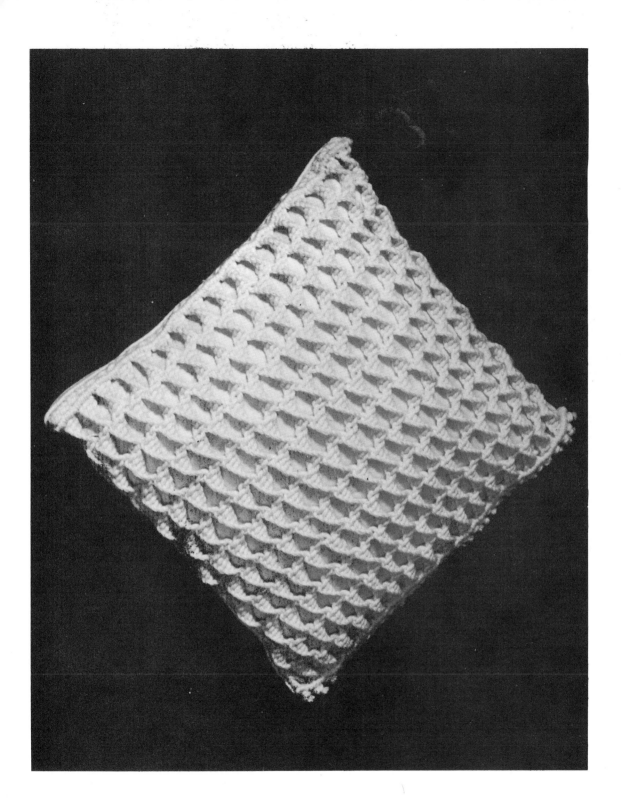

SQUARE CUSHION WITH FRINGE

This cushion is worked from the centre outwards, in double-double knitting wool, and the lines of vertical half hitching are worked in a random dyed wood of the same weight. This is one of the few ways of using this sort of wool in macramé work, as usually the mixed colours destroy the knotted pattern.

Measurements
36 cm (14 in.) square, with a 7.5 cm (3 in.) fringe all round

Materials
2 *Suisses Weekend* 100 gr (4 oz) balls of double-double knitting wool in white
Approximately 11 m (12 yd) of random dyed wool of the same thickness. The one used here is a heather-mixture mohair.

Cut in white
Sixteen 165 cm (5½ ft) lengths
Sixteen 135 cm (4½ ft) lengths
Odd lengths for attached leaders

The pattern
1 Divide the threads into groups of four, two short and two long. Lay ends level at one end, and measure 60 cm (2 ft) from this point. Work a sinnet of 7.5 cm (3 in.) of flat knots, using the longer ones as knotting threads.

2 Weave the 8 sinnets together into a tight square, and pin on the board.

3 Using an attached white leader make a row of horizontal cording all round the square, finishing by cording one end of the leader on to the other. Pull the ends of the leader through to the back.

4 Using 180 cm (2 yd) of the random dyed wool, make two rows of vertical double half hitches all round.

Cut
Twelve 135 cm (4½ ft) lengths of white wool and repeat step 3, setting-on three doubled threads to the leader at each corner with double half hitches.

5 Make a flat knot with the six corner threads. Between the corners, divide the threads each side into two groups of eight, and make flat knots over four core threads with a pair of knotting threads each side.

Cut
Sixteen 105 cm (3½ ft) lengths of white wool, and repeat step 3, setting the doubled threads on to the leader with double half hitches, two in the middle of each corner flat knot, and one each side.

6 Using 360 cm (4 yd) of random dyed wool, work a row of vertical double half hitches all round.

Cut
Eight 105 cm (3½ ft) lengths of white wool and repeat step 3, setting them on doubled, two at each corner, with double half hitches.

7 Work two rows of alternate flat knots.

Cut
Eight threads 90 cm (3 ft) long, and set them on to the knotting threads at each corner, as shown in figure 60.

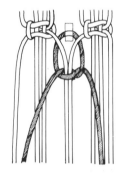

60 Adding threads to flat knots

8 Work three rows of alternate flat knots.

Cut
Eight 30 cm (1 ft) lengths of white wool and repeat step 3, setting-on 2 doubled threads with double half hitches at each corner.
Repeat step 6 with 5.5 m (6 yd) of random dyed wool.

Repeat step 3, adding some doubled 20 cm (8 in.) lengths of white wool at the corners if necessary. Cord one end of the leader over the other, and leave ends to be included in the fringe.

To finish Trim all ends 7.5 cm (3 in.) from
the last row of cording. Sew in the ends of the
attached leaders.

Sew the square on a square cushion cover.

CUSHION USING PATTERNS FROM SAMPLER 3

Measurements
38 cm (15 in.) square

Materials
156 m (170 yd) of *Atlas Bulkycord* or *Patons Turkey* rug wool
1 cushion cover 38 cm (15 in.) square
1 cushion pad to fit

Cut
Thirty-six 420 cm (14 ft) lengths, and three 60 cm (2 ft) lengths for holding cord and leaders.

Note: this is a very wasteful pattern, as some knots use a great deal more yarn than others. However the exact calculated lengths are so complicated, and depend upon keeping every single strand in its right place all through the pattern, that only one length has been given for all threads.

Set-on 36 doubled lengths with lark's head knots.

The pattern
1 With attached leader, work a row of horizontal cording across all threads.

2 First 40 threads. Work 7 rows of alternate flat knots
Next 4 threads. Work 8 flat knots with picots
Next 12 threads. Work flat knot with a pair of threads each side over the central 8
Next 4 threads. Work 8 flat knots with picots
Last 12 threads. Work a single diagonal cross, then work two more crosses down the length.

3 Start again, and using the first thread as leader work a row of horizontal cording across the next 59 threads. Check that all the threads are in their right order.

Divide these 60 threads into groups of four, and work 2 flat knots on each group. Using the last (60th) thread as leader, make a row of horizontal cording from right to left over 59 threads.

4 Start again.

First 24 threads. Work a diamond in triple diagonal cording, making a central flat knot over 12 core threads with three knotting threads each side.
Next 4 threads. Make 12 flat knots with picots
Next 32 threads. Work berry knots for 5 alternate rows

Line up the berry knots, the flat knot sinnet with picots, and the length of diagonal crosses at the end. If they are not level, add or subtract knots as needed. Then, using last thread as leader, work a row of horizontal cording to the left over 47 threads.

Divide this 48-thread group into groups of 6 threads. In each group, using the last thread as leader, cord it diagonally to the left over 5 threads.

5 Start again.

Using the first thread as leader make a row of horizontal cording over all threads from left to right.

First 32 threads. Work 7 rows of alternate sinnets of 5 half knots
Next 4 threads. Work a sinnet of 12 flat knots with picots
Next 36 threads. Divide into groups of four and make a flat knot ball of four flat knots on each

Using last thread as leader, make a row of horizontal cording from right to left across 35 threads. In the same group of 36, divide group work a diamond centred with a flat knot, crossing neighbouring leaders. Using the last thread as leader, work a row of horizontal cording from right to left over 35 threads. Divide these 36 threads into groups of 4. Make a double knotted chain on each group.

Use the last thread as leader, and work a row of horizontal cording across all threads from right to left. Repeat from * to * once more.

To finish Trim ends, turn them under, and sew them into the back of the work.

Sew the knotted square on to the cushion cover.

PATTERNED CUSHION IN TWO COLOURS

Measurements
40 cm x 30 cm (16 in. x 12 in.)

Materials
Double-double knitting wool
Dark colour — one 100 gram (4 oz) ball
Light colour — two 100 gram (4 oz) balls

Cut
Dark colour — Fourteen 360 cm (4 yd) lengths
Light colour — Sixteen 360 cm (4 yd) lengths,
twelve 270 cm (3 yd) lengths, three lengths of
50 cm (20 in.) for holding cord and attached
leaders.

Set-on doubled to a holding cord as follows:
One dark, four light 360 cm (4 yd), (two
dark, two light 270 cm (3 yd), two light 360
cm (4 yd)) five times. Two dark, four light
270 cm (3 yd), one dark.

The pattern is worked from the longest side.

1 Using an attached leader, work one row of
horizontal cording

2 Divide the light threads into groups of four,
and work one flat knot on each group.

Make a single knotted chain on each pair of
dark threads.

3 Using the light threads as leaders, cord them
out in groups of four to right and left over
two dark threads.

4 Dark threads — make a single knotted chain
on each pair.

Combine adjoining pairs to make a double
knotted chain, then re-divide into the
original pairs and make a single knotted
chain on each.

Light threads — with the first four and the
last four threads in the row, use the inner
one as leader to cord to the edge and back
again.
Work a berry knot with all other groups of
eight threads. Repeat steps 3 and 4 until
the pattern is the required length. Repeat
step 1. Take the knotting off the board, pin,
and then sew on to the cushion cover.

Flat knot sinnet surrounding cushion. Cut
two core threads long enough to encircle the
cushion with 15 cm (6 in.) to spare, and four
knotting threads 7.5 m (8 yd) long. Knot them
together at one end, and work flat knots with
doubled knotting threads for the required
length.

To finish Pin the sinnet in place, weaving in
the ends where they meet, then sew round
the cushion.

BELTS

Many of the braids and sinnets in this book will make up into belts. Lark's head braids in thick yarns are one of the quickest and easiest ways of knotting a belt. Narrow sinnets can always be applied to suede or leather or canvas, and various kinds of sinnets with picots can be sewn to a backing. A round rope belt can be made entirely of Chinese crown knots, or a narrow strip of cavandoli work can be mounted on a petersham ribbon — however both these methods take quite a long time.

Yarns Choose a firm strong yarn, without too much 'give' in it. Belts use long lengths, so that soft yarns tend to pull apart and those with a wrapped core begin to unravel. The amount of elasticity in a yarn is important — if you suspect that your chosen yarn will stretch, use a pattern like the double lark's head braid which is worked on two rigid core threads.

Technique Belts are worked in sections on the knotting board. They can be started from an overhand knot, and finished in the same way. They can be set-on to a buckle bar with lark's head knots. Some belts can be started from a ring in the middle with set-on threads, and lengths worked both ways.

Lengths If an average waist is 60 cm (24 in.), then eight times that is more than 450 cm (5 yd), so it will be seen that making a belt involves the management of a considerable length of yarn. Wind the long ends into figure-of-eight hanks, starting from the end nearest the work, and secure them with a rubber band. Draw out amounts of yarn as they are required. Reckon on about 6 m (6 yd) doubled for most kinds of belt, and anywhere from four to twelve set-on threads.

Finishing To knot the end of a belt on the other end of the buckle to match the lark's head knots at the beginning, work as follows: Divide the threads into pairs. Pass each pair in turn over the buckle bar from front to back. Separate the ends, and then pass them through to the front again on either side. Cross the ends in front, pass them through to the back again on either side. At the back either sew the ends in, make a flat knot, or make an overhand knot, depending on the type of yarn.

TWO-COLOUR BELT IN LARK'S HEAD BRAID

On the left in the photograph on page 73

Measurements
65 cm (26 in.)
2.5 cm (1 in.) wide

Materials
Novacord 2.5 mm (⅛ in.) wide. 9 m (10 yd) each of two colours, A and B
One figure-of-eight clasp

Clasp
Two 450 cm (5 yd) lengths of each colour

Set-on to the clasp with lark's head knots in the following order:
One colour A length folded 360 cm and 90 cm (4 yd and 1 yd)
One colour A length folded 90 cm and 360 cm (1 yd and 4 yd)
One colour B length folded 360 cm and 90 cm (4 yd and 1 yd)
One colour B length folded 90 cm and 360 cm (1 yd and 4 yd)

The pattern
Make a flat knot with each group of colours. The core threads should be the short lengths. Work in double lark's head braid for the required length, as shown in figure 61.

To finish Knot the threads on to the other end of the clasp as described under belts, *finishing*.

Plate 1 Plant hanger in thick yarn, instructions page 34
Sprang hanging, instructions page 96
Shopping bag, instructions page 109
Shoulder bag with cavandoli initialled flap,
instructions page 113

Plate 2 Narrow gold collar, instructions page 56
Silver and gold cavandoli watch strap, instructions
page 88
Christmas stars in Lustrecord, instructions page 61

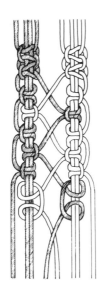

61 A double lark's head braid

STRING BELT WITH DOUBLE BUCKLE

At the bottom in the photograph on page 73

Measurements
60 cm (24 in.) long
5 cm (2 in.) wide

Materials
46 cm (50 yd) of 1.5 mm (¹/₁₆ in.) *Cotton Seine Twine*
A buckle in two halves

Cut
Eight 540 cm (6 yd) lengths

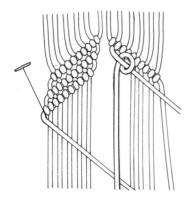

62 A triple diagonal corded diamond

Set-on to the buckle bar of one half of the buckle, doubled, with lark's head knots.

The pattern
This is just a triple diagonal cross, with a multiple flat knot in between, and a sinnet of flat knots each side.

1 Work the first half of the triple cross.

2 Make a sinnet of four flat knots with the first and last four threads.

3 Complete the second half of the triple cross.

4 Leave the two leaders aside. Make a flat knot over the central eight threads with four threads each side.

Repeat steps 1 to 4 for the required length. If some threads become short, it is possible to re-arrange the threads as they come out of the multiple flat knot and substitute longer ones. Finish on a pattern that matches the first one.

To finish Divide the threads into pairs, and knot them to the buckle bar of the other half of the buckle, as described on page 72 (see belts, *finishing*).

THREE-COLOUR BELT WITH ANCHOR BUCKLE

On the right in the photograph on page 73

Measurements
66 cm (26 in.) long
4 cm (1½ in. wide

Materials
Three colours of *Tubular Rayon Cord* 2 mm (¹/₁₆ in.) wide. The belt in the photograph is red, white and blue
18.5 m (20 yd) of each colour

Cut
Colour A   Four 450 cm (5 yd) lengths
B and C   Two 900 cm (10 yd) lengths each

Set-on doubled to the buckle bar, with lark's head knots, in the following order: 2A 1B 2C 1B 2A (see figure 63)

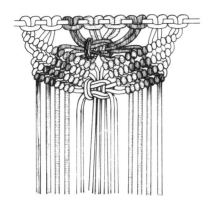

63 Three-colour corded pattern for a belt

The pattern

1 Make a flat knot over the central four C threads with a pair of B threads each side.

2 Cord all four outside A threads into the centre.

3 Make a flat knot over the four central A threads with a pair of A threads each side.

4 Cord the groups of four A threads out to the side again.

Repeat steps 1 to 4 for the required length.

To finish Knot the ends over the other end of the buckle as described on page 72 (see belts, *finishing*).

WIDE BELT WITH TWO CLASPS

At the top in the photograph on page 73.

Measurements
60 cm (24 in.) long. 7.5 cm (3 in.) wide

Materials
64 m (70 yd) of *Rayon Cord* 3 mm (1/8 in.) wide
Two clasps

Cut
Ten 540 cm (6 yd) lengths
Two 450 cm (5 yd) lengths

Set-on five doubled 540 cm (6 yd.) lengths to each half of two clasps, with lark's head knots.

The pattern

1 For each clasp work as follows: using the first thread as leader, work two rows of horizontal cording. Work a double diagonal cross with all threads.

2 Use one of the 450 cm (5 yd) lengths as an attached leader, and work a row of cording across both strips. At the end of the row, add the other 450 cm (5 yd) length with a double half hitch (keep the thread single, not double, and sew the short end into the back). Using the same leader, work another row of horizontal cording.

3 There are now twelve hanging threads. Work in double alternate flat knots for the required length, remembering that the narrow strips at the other end are going to add 9 cm (3½ in.). Make a buttonhole edge by using the long threads at the side to work three vertical half hitches on the idle threads on alternate rows.

4 Work two rows of horizontal cording across all threads, using first or last threads as leader. Leave these two threads idle and sew them into the back afterwards. Divide the work into two groups of 10 threads, and work two more strips to match the ones at the beginning.

To finish Divide the threads into pairs, and attach them to the complementary halves of the clasps as described on page 72.

THREE DIMENSIONAL WORK

Knotting can be used to cover bottles and tins and so on, to convert them to more decorative uses such as lamp bases and waste-paper baskets. Other items such as goldfish bowls and fern cases can be suspended in sinnets like planters. More mundane objects such as loudspeakers can simply be slung up to keep them out of the way.

Lampshades are another kind of three-dimensional work, done on a frame, but the same technique with separate rings and stiffer yarns and wooden bases can be used to make baskets like the one on the table in colour plate 4. Knotting can be open, like the basket or the flagon on page 77, or closely corded like the bottle on page 80. Although the cording is worked over a bottle, using *Raffene* over a string leader, if the string were replaced by flex or plastic tubing the shape would stand up on its own and could be worked freely.

Yarns For an open pattern, string or cotton are the easiest to manage, as they do not slip. A close-corded pattern on the other hand, wraps securely round the object and can be worked in any kind of yarn. If you are covering something that really is going to get wet, a practical choice is one of the various grades of polypropylene parcel twine. It is stiff and springy and not at all easy to use, but the result is effective, shiny and washable and unlikely to rot.

Lengths The general rule of eight times the length of the knotting can be used. Close cording will need about ten times. Long sinnets will need longer knotting threads — work a sample and see how much extra it needs. Any areas of vertical half hitching use an extra amount of yarn. The easiest pattern to start with is alternate flat knots, using the average length of yarn and setting on doubled threads, and the pattern will fit almost any shape if the distance between the knots and rows is varied.

Methods Most covers start from the top, though it is possible to work from a ring taped to the base. The work can be secured during progress by sticking the knots to the container with little bits of sellotape. Long sinnets may have to be glued in place down the back. Extra threads can be added to leaders with reversed lark's head knots (*see* figure 64), or double half hitches (*see* figure 52), or doubled threads can be added to flat knots, as in figure 60.

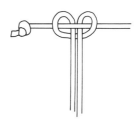

64 A reversed lark's head knot

GENERAL INSTRUCTIONS FOR COVERING A STRAIGHT-SIDED CONTAINER

Begin by cutting a holding cord long enough to go round the container three times plus 15 cm (6 in.). Cut a number of threads eight times the length of the knotting, plus a few cm/in., double them, and set them on to one end of the holding cord. Loop the latter round the top of the object, add more doubled threads if necessary, but check that the final number of hanging threads is divisible by four. Cord one end of the holding cord over the other where it meets, and tuck the short end under the subsequent rows of cording. Using the holding cord as a leader, work a couple of rows of cording all round. Paint clear glue under this heading, and glue it in place round the top of the container before continuing in the chosen pattern.

Finish with a couple of rows of cording, and dispose of the ends in any of the following ways: cut them off close to the cording and glue the latter round the bottom of the container. Leave about 2.5 cm (1 in.) of ends, turn them under and glue them to the base. Make an overhand knot over each end or pair of ends, trim closely and paint them over with clear glue.

BOTTLE COVERED WITH AN OPEN PATTERN IN STRING

Measurements
30 cm (12 in.) high, 53 cm (21 in.) round the widest part, base 9 cm (3½ in.)
The bottle is a 2.5 l (½ gal) cider flagon

Materials
128 m (140 yd) of medium 1.5 mm (¹/₁₆ in.) wide *Cotton Seine Twine* (more if your bottle is bigger)

Cut
One 180 cm (6 ft) length for a holding cord and leader
Twenty-two 300 cm (10 ft) lengths
Twelve 240 cm (8 ft) lengths
Sixteen 180 cm (6 ft) lengths

Set-on The 180 cm (6 ft) length is used both as a holding cord and a leader. Double the twenty-two 300 cm (10 ft) lengths and set them on to the holding cord at one end with lark's head knots. (If your bottle is bigger than this one, set-on more, but make sure it is a number divisible by four). Loop the holding cord round the top of the neck just under the lip and cord one end over the other. The short end can be tucked under the cording as it is worked. Use the long end to work two tight rows of horizontal cording round the neck.

The pattern

1 Divide the threads into groups of four (excluding the leader). Make sinnets of five flat knots, bringing the leader down to the next level by incorporating it in the core threads of the nearest sinnet. Hold sinnets in place with bits of sellotape.

2 Using the same leader, work two rows of horizontal cording.

3 Divide the threads into groups of four, and work sinnets of six half knots that spiral once. Bring the leader down in the same way.

4 With the same leader, work a row of horizontal cording, setting-on one doubled 240 cm (8 ft) thread in between each sinnet, with a reversed lark's head knot. The last addition is where the cording meets. Then cord over the next two threads to secure the join.

5 Divide the threads into groups of four and work sinnets of twelve half knots that spiral twice, bringing the leader thread down as before.

6 Using the same leader, work a row of horizontal cording, setting on one doubled 180 cm (6 ft) thread with reversed lark's head knots in between each sinnet except the last. Work another row of cording. The leader is not used again; trim the end, dip it in clear glue, and tuck it behind the cording.

7 Work in a pattern of alternate flat knots for about eight rows, around 12 cm (5 in.) from the bottom. The spacing between the rows and the knots will increase with the girth of the bottle.

8 Divide the threads into groups of four and work sinnets of flat knots to within 2.5 cm (1 in.) of the bottom.

9 Using the longest remaining thread as leader, work a row of horizontal cording, pressing the knotting down over the bottle until the ends meet. Continue to cord round the bottle, pulling the leader tightly, making a close band round the bottom. If your bottle diminishes in diameter very quickly, it may be necessary to leave some threads idle as you work so that the cording may fit tightly.

To finish Within about 10 mm (¼ in.) of the bottom cut the ends so that they just reach the base, brush them with clear glue, and stroke them into place, as shown in the photograph.

SISAL BASKET

(See colour plate 4 facing page 97)

Measurements
10 cm (4 in.) high. 20 cm (8 in.) diameter

Materials
One 20 cm (8 in.) circular wood base (for canework)
Two 20 cm (8 in.) metal lampshade rings
138 m (151 yd) of thick sisal 4 mm (³/₁₆ in.) wide

Cut
Seventy-five 180 cm (2 yd) lengths
One 45 cm (18 in.) length for attached leader

Set-on the 75 doubled lengths on to a ring with lark's head knots

The pattern

1 Using the attached leader, work a row of horizontal cording all round — (leave both ends of the leader inside the ring and sew them into the back afterwards).

2 Work in alternate flat knots for 10 cm (4 in.)

3 Make double half hitches on to the other ring with all threads.

4 Divide threads into groups of 12. In each group work a pattern of diminishing rows of alternate flat knots (3 rows). *Cord first and last thread into the centre, cording one across the other at the point.* Repeat from * to * once.

To finish Turn under all ends and sew into the back with a strong thread. Turn the petals outwards, and sew the point of each to the basket.

Fasten the ring to the wooden base with wire, passed over the ring and through the holes in the base, and spread out on the underside of the base. A circle of felt can be glued over to cover the wire.

BOTTLE COVERED WITH CLOSE CORDING

Measurements
23 cm (9 in.) high. 7.5 cm (3 in.) across the base

Materials
A bottle
4 hanks of different coloured *Raffene* (A B C D)
String — the bottle illustrated used 2 m (2 yd) approximately of fine string as a leader for the cording. If your bottle is larger use at least 4 m (4 yd) or draw it from the ball

Cut
3 lengths of colour A ⎤ Ten times the height of
7 lengths of colour B ⎬ your bottle, and more
9 lengths of colour C ⎦ lengths if required for
a larger one

Set-on the doubled lengths to the string, keeping them in colour groups. Add more if required; they should fit comforably round the neck of the bottle. Loop the string round just under the lip, and cord one end over the other. Leave the short end to be covered with the cording as it progresses.

The pattern consists simply of cording round and round the bottle, using the string as a leader. As shown in the photograph, it can be gripped between the knees, and the string drawn from a ball on the floor. As the bottle widens add more doubled threads, each ten times the height of the remaining area. Set them on to the string with reversed lark's head knots. At this point add in colour D, starting with one doubled thread and adding another in each subsequent row, so that the new colour band widens as it flows down and

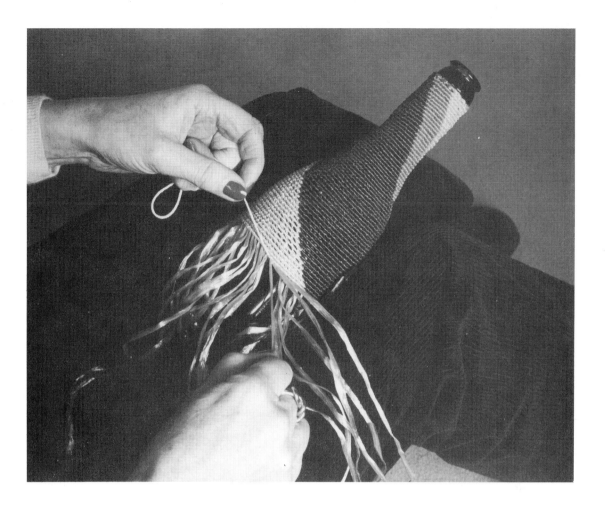

round the bottle. It is easy to tell when new threads are needed, as the threads begin to slope backwards, and it becomes difficult to cover all the string.

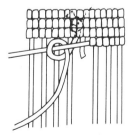

65 Replacing a thread in close cording round a bottle

If a *Raffene* end gets too short or breaks, replace it as in figure 65. Cut another length in the right colour, make a tiny knot one end and dip it in clear glue. Push it up under the knotting in the right place and cord the length on to the leader as it passes. Trim the replaced end and glue it to the bottle.

To finish take the cording right down to the very bottom edge. Most bottles have an indented base, so cut the ends to about 2.5 cm (1 in.) and stroke them up inside the base with a finger dipped in clear glue. If the base of the bottle is flat, you can still glue on the *Raffene* as it is so fine — however, if you are using a thicker yarn, finish short of the bottom and glue the ends there, or glue the last line of cording in place.

FRINGES

One of the best ways of using macramé is to make fringes. A great variety of yarns can be used, some of which can be seen on page 85. They add a decorative touch to all sorts of items, and do not involve a great deal of work. They are worked in sections across the board, so there are only a few threads set-on at any one time, and even very simple patterns make a nice effect.

General method of working a fringe
Lengths Cut a holding cord, and leaders for the rows of horizontal cording, long enough for the required amount of fringe, plus a few cm/in. Measure the depth of fringe required, multiply by eight, and cut enough lengths for one motif, or about 15 cm (6 in.) of fringe. (After that you will be able to see how much yarn has been used, and can calculate more accurately.)

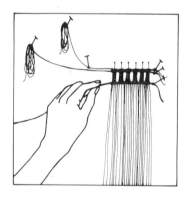

66a Method of setting up a fringe

Method Start on the right side of the board, (unless you are left-handed it is always easier to work from right to left.) Make a knot at one end of the holding cord and pin it to the board. Make a loose knot further on and pin the cord in a horizontal line; loop the rest out of the way. Double the short lengths and set them on to the holding cord with lark's head knots. Make an overhand knot at one end of an attached leader, pin it under the holding cord knot, and cord across the

hanging threads. Loop the leader temporarily out of the way. Pin each set-on thread into place to make a firm heading. Work the first motif, or the first few cm/in. of the fringe. Set-on more threads, and work the next section. Continue in this way until the fringe is the required length.

To finish If the fringe is circular, such as a fringe round a lampshade, it will need to be joined invisibly at the back. Before doing this, pin the fringe round the lamp frame or whatever and check that it is the right length. If the join falls between two motifs, work another one. It is better to make the fringe too long than too short, as it can be slightly gathered along the holding cord.

Joining a fringe
Lay the beginning and the end of the fringe face downwards on the board. Using a crochet hook, pull one end of the holding cord through the cording on the other side, then

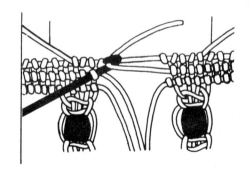

66b Joining a fringe

pull the other end of the holding cord through the cording on the opposite side. Do the same with the attached leaders. Pull each end of the holding cord and leaders until the fringe meets. Sew all the ends into the back.

Trimming a fringe
For best results work in sections as follows: measure the required depth of the fringe.

Ideas for fringes, braids and motifs

Draw a line across the knotting board this distance from the edge. Pin the top of the fringe across this line, making sure it does not sag between the pins. Smooth all the threads down, hold the board at an angle so that they hang vertically and evenly off the edge of the board. Cut cleanly across the bottom of the board with a sharp long-bladed pair of scissors.

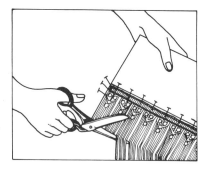

66c Trimming a fringe

FRINGES, BRAIDS AND MOTIFS

A A soft silky fringe in tubular rayon cord — similar to the one on the tiffany lamp and round the table in the colour photograph 4 facing page 97. This kind of fringe, with finer beads, can also be used to edge a shawl or jacket or skirt (figure 67).

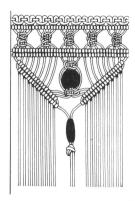

67 The motif for the fringe in colour plate 4

B An idea for a deep fringe in tubular rayon cord for the end of a scarf.

C A decorative strap with beads. The sample here is made in metal embroidery threads (*Schurer SI*) with small glass beads, black in the centre and gold at the edges. On a larger scale this pattern makes interesting bracelets or chokers or hairbands. It is worked entirely in cording, and will change in appearance according to the size and shape of the chosen beads. It is not a pattern recommended for working in great lengths, however, because of the tedium of threading three beads on every single row. The method is as follows:

Cut
5 threads 8 times the length required.

Set-on doubled, to a short holding cord, and work two rows of cording with the last threads.

Row 1 Pass the first, last, and two centre threads through a bead, as shown in figure 68a.

Row 2 Using the first and last threads as leaders, cord them diagonally into the centre, each over four threads, as shown in figure 68b, and 68c.

Repeat rows 1 and 2 for the required length.

To finish Work a few rows of diagonal cording into the centre, crossing leaders at the point. Either knot the ends off in pairs, or sew them into the back of the work.

D and O Two ideas for a fringe in raffia (synthetic raffia comes in a beautiful range of colours, and in long lengths of regular width). Although raffia makes a stiff fringe, it is quite suitable to go on something like a waste paper basket, and is useful for beachwear and accessories.

E and G These cavandoli straps are made in crochet cotton (*Twilleys Lisbet*), and were designed for watch straps. (Instructions on how to make watch straps can be found under the section on cavandoli). Wider straps could be used on evening bags, or as belts, chokers, hairbands and dress trimmings. Longer narrow lengths can be used as braids, like the ones on the cushion on page 63. On the whole it is better to use cavandoli braids in small amounts, as they are somewhat tedious to work.

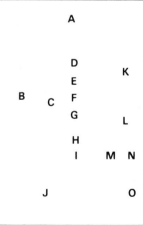

```
            A


         D           K
         E
B     C  F
         G
         H
         I        M  N

   J                    O
```

F A flower shape — basically the same as the
  petal frame on page 116 without the vertical
  half hitching line round. This tiny motif is
  made in fine crochet cotton, centred with a
  bead and a large sequin. It could be used
  on a greetings card, or for the Christmas
  tree, or the top of a box — or in many of
  the ways sketched in the section on
  flowers and butterflies.

H An edging in alternate berry knots. The
  other way up, worked in soft yarn, it
  could be a fringe — in thicker yarn it
  might be a pelmet, or in very fine yarn
  an edging. The way it is shown, worked
  in *Lustrecord*, it could be used for a circlet for a bridesmaid, as shown in the
  sketch on page 83. Beads could be added
  at the end of the berry knots. If working

in *Lustrecord*, finish the ends of the knots with clear nail varnish, as described for the collar in the jewellery section.

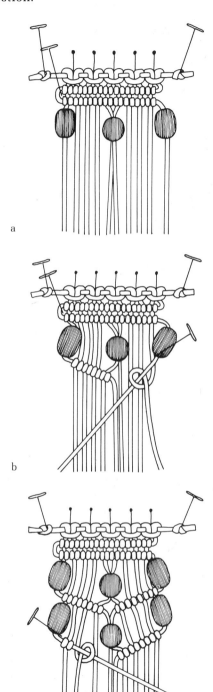

a

b

c

68 Braid – see (C) in photograph on page 85

I   This is 'angling' as described in figure 78. It is worked in raffia, with two colours interlaced.

J   A thick fringe in *Bulkycord*. A length of random coloured tweedy knitting wool was used for the row of vertical half hitches, and to wrap alternate tassels. This fringe could be used for curtains, or as a pelmet, or a valance — or in finer yarn as the hem of a long skirt.

K   A light and floaty fringe consisting of a mixture of wool, rayon, silk and cotton yarns, incorporating small feathers. These are knotted into the fringe in the following way: strip some of the down from the shaft of the feather, and dip the end in clear glue. Lay the shaft along one of the threads in the chosen position, and use another thin thread to make a wrapping over them both (*see* figure 48). A free-floating fringe like this might be the making of a fashionable shawl.

L   A *Lustrecord* beaded fringe with a thick crusty jewelled look about it. A decoration for an evening bag perhaps, or an evening cloak, or a flamboyant trimming for a stage costume.

M   A simple braid in three colours in alternate flat knots, with a buttonholed edge. It could be used as a strap for a bag, or as a belt, or in fine cotton as a dress trimming.

N   This motif in fine crochet thread could be made into a delicate collar, or, on a much larger scale, into a pelmet or trimming for a curtain.

CAVANDOLI WORK

This may seem at first sight to be a limited technique, but it is possible to achieve a surprising variety of different effects. Cavandoli work can be substituted in many instances where canvas work is now used, such as covering chair seats and stools, and it makes excellent rugs. It is much quicker to work than tapestry, and does not require an expensive painted canvas. There is also scope for cavandoli work in church furnishings, making kneelers and chair pads and small rugs. In fine yarn, cavandoli work can become narrow braid. Small areas of cavandoli work can be incorporated into ordinary knotting, like the flap of the bag (see figure 87). Cavandoli could also be used for the headings of curtains or pelmets, and in a free way it can be alternated with rows of sinnets.

Yarns Choose a smooth, strong, easy-running yarn. It should be able to stand up to the strain of being knotted so closely, and yet be soft enough to result in a pliable fabric. Rug wools, *Bulkycord, Tubular Rayon Cord,* all kinds of jute and cotton can be used successfully. Fine braids can be made of silk, metal and linen threads, crochet cottons and fine wools. The pattern thread is often the same as the background thread but of a different colour. It should be the same weight if it is a different yarn, but it is interesting to experiment with contrasting textures.

Lengths In general, background threads need to be ten times the length of the finished piece. Pattern threads vary in length according to the amount of colour in the pattern, but are rarely less than three times the length of the background threads. There is no need to start off with the whole amount, however, as extra amounts can easily be added, as shown in figure 69. If background threads run out, they also are easy to replace, as shown in figure 70.

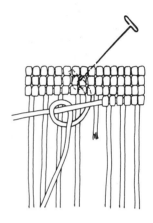

70 Replacing a short background thread

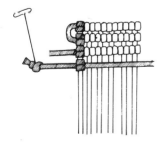

69 Adding a new length of pattern thread

HOW TO DESIGN A PATTERN FOR CAVANDOLI WORK

Patterns are planned on graph paper, like cross stitch or canvas work. However, it should be remembered that in cavandoli work the blank squares are horizontal cording (knots side by side), and the crossed squares are vertical cording (knots one above the other), so that the final result works out longer and narrower than it appears on the graph paper. Also, only two colours are used, so that no shading is possible, and one has to think of motifs as silhouettes.

Decide on the measurements of the item you are going to make. Make a sample with the chosen yarn, setting-on at least six doubled threads to a short holding cord, and working 2.5 cm (1 in.) of horizontal corded rows. Measure across the hanging threads to find the number to the inch, then multiply by the width of your design, and this gives you the number of squares across the top of the pattern. Measure the number of rows of horizontal cording to the cm/in., multiply by the depth of your design, and this gives you the number of squares from top to bottom of your pattern. (In the case of a braid, just make it long enough for one repeat pattern). Draw a line round the shape on your graph paper. Mark the centre line both ways. Plan your pattern from the centre out. If you are copying a shape or flower, work with transparent (tracing) graph paper and lay it over the chosen shape and work crosses over it.

As this is a geometrical method, curves will be stepped, and circles will be somewhat squared. Try not to use single lines of vertical half hitching, as they always look a bit wobbly. Work in blocks and shapes and keep it fairly simple.

GENERAL INSTRUCTIONS FOR CAVANDOLI WATCH STRAPS

Base the width and length on the old watch strap, and measure the distance between the bar on the watch and the buckle bar. On the whole, watch straps are too narrow for more than a simple repeating motif, or stripes or checks, but it is possible to incorporate initials.

The watch strap (E) on page 85 was worked in crochet cotton. See figure 71 for the graph to be used for this watch strap. The watch strap in colour plate 2 facing page 73 was worked in silver metal thread (*Schurer SI*) with the gold as a pattern thread. The

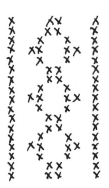

71 Graph for watch strap (E) on page 85

pattern is stripes, 4 rows of silver, 2 rows of gold and the pattern thread is turned at the edges with no picots.

Materials
Two colours of linen thread, crochet cotton, or similar fine, smooth, twisted thread. The buckle of the old strap, or a new small buckle. (In shops these are sometimes called 'sandal' buckles.)

*Cut
The number of background threads required by the pattern, each 120 cm (4 ft) long. One length of pattern thread in another colour about 3 m (3 yd) long.

Set-on doubled background threads with lark's head knots to the bar of the watch. Pin the pattern thread end to the left side as shown in the cavandoli sampler, figure 37. Work in pattern for the measured length from the watch bar to the buckle bar*. Pass the ends over the buckle bar and sew them in at the back. To make the tapered end of the strap, repeat from * to * once. Check on the fit, and add another motif or two if required before the strap starts to taper — from which point it will extend about another 2.5 cm (1 in.).

Taper the strap as follows: continue to make picots at the side, but make the first vertical knots in each row over *two* threads instead of one, and pin the outside thread to one side (as in figures 72a and b). As the width diminishes, reduce the pattern in size if it consists of motifs, or leave them out altogether. (If the pattern is just stripes these can be continued to the end). When the last two threads are reached, make two vertical half hitches over them with the pattern thread, then turn all these last ends under and sew them into the back.

To finish Sew in all the loose threads at the sides, and trim and sew in the end of the pattern thread.

Try on the strap, and mark the point where the spike of the buckle should pierce it. Push a blunt-pointed instrument through between the threads to make a round hole, and oversew the edges.

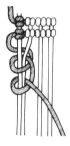 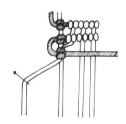

72a Tapering a strap, stage 1   **72b Tapering a strap, stage 2**

CAVANDOLI STOOL COVER

Measurements
30 cm (12 in.) square

Materials
Thick yarn, width 5 mm (³/₁₆ in.)
Patons Turkey rug wool, or *Bulkycord*
85 m (92 yd) of background colour
46 m (50 yd) of pattern colour

Cut in background colour
Eighteen 270 cm (9 ft) lengths
Ten 330 cm (11 ft) lengths
A holding cord 45 cm (18 in.) long

The shaped pattern
The stool cover in the photograph is shaped at the corners to accommodate the legs of the stool.

Set-on doubled threads to the holding cord with double half hitches in the following order: three 330 cm (11 ft) lengths, eighteen 270 cm (9 ft) lengths, three 330 cm (11 ft) lengths.

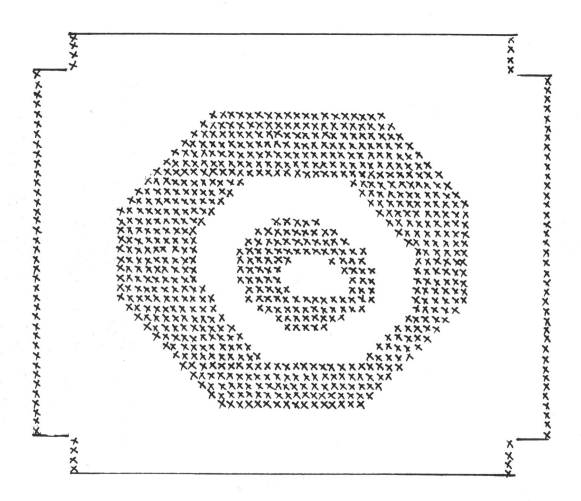

Use a pattern thread only long enough to work the first three rows. At the fourth row use a longer pattern thread, and set two doubled 330 cm (11 ft) lengths with double half hitches on to it at the beginning and end of the row. Continue in pattern to within four rows of the end, then leave aside four threads at the beginning and end of the row.

A square pattern
To work a simple square, set the doubled threads on to the holding cord with double half hitches in the following order: five 330 cm (11 ft) lengths, eighteen 270 cm (9 ft) lengths, five 330 cm (11 ft) lengths.

Work in pattern, following the graph, making picots at each side, for the required length.

To finish Trim all ends to about 2 cm (³/₄ in.), turn them under and sew them into the back.

CAVANDOLI LAMPSHADE

Doubled threads are set on to a lampshade ring and worked in a cavandoli pattern that separates into eight petals. If using a different yarn or another size of ring, set on threads in multiples of twelve in order to fit the pattern.

Measurements
25 cm (10 in.) diameter. Each petal is 19 cm (7½ in.) deep plus fringe

Materials
One 25 cm (10 in.) diameter lampshade ring with light fitting
147 m (160 yd) of a light-coloured *Tubular Rayon Cord*
69 m (75 yd) of dark-coloured *Rayon Cord*

The pattern
This is shown in the graph. Each motif is 24 threads across (twelve set-on doubled threads).

Cut
Ninety six 150 cm (5 ft) lengths of the light colour.

Set-on doubled to the ring with lark's head knots.

Work in cavandoli knotting, using the dark colour as leader, following the graph.

Trim the fringe to the required length.

To finish Sew in the ends of the dark cord.

NURSERY RUG IN CAVANDOLI

Worked in *Bulkycord* in two colours, one dark and one light, from a graph of Noah's Ark and two doves.

Measurements
55 cm by 100 cm (22 in. by 40 in.) including fringe

Materials
Light-coloured *Bulkycord* 391 m (427 yd)
Dark-coloured *Bulkycord* 125 m (136 yd)

Cut in the light colour
Twenty-four 1080 cm (12 yd) lengths
Sixteen 780 cm (8 yd 2 ft) lengths
The dark colour is used as the pattern colour

Set-on by hanging the folded threads on pins, as shown in figure 51 for the tablemats, and

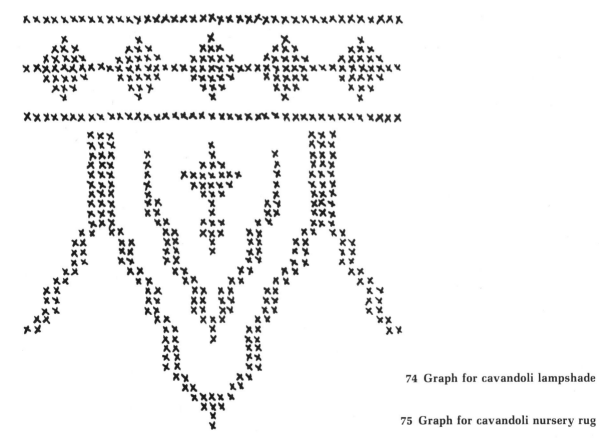

74 Graph for cavandoli lampshade

75 Graph for cavandoli nursery rug

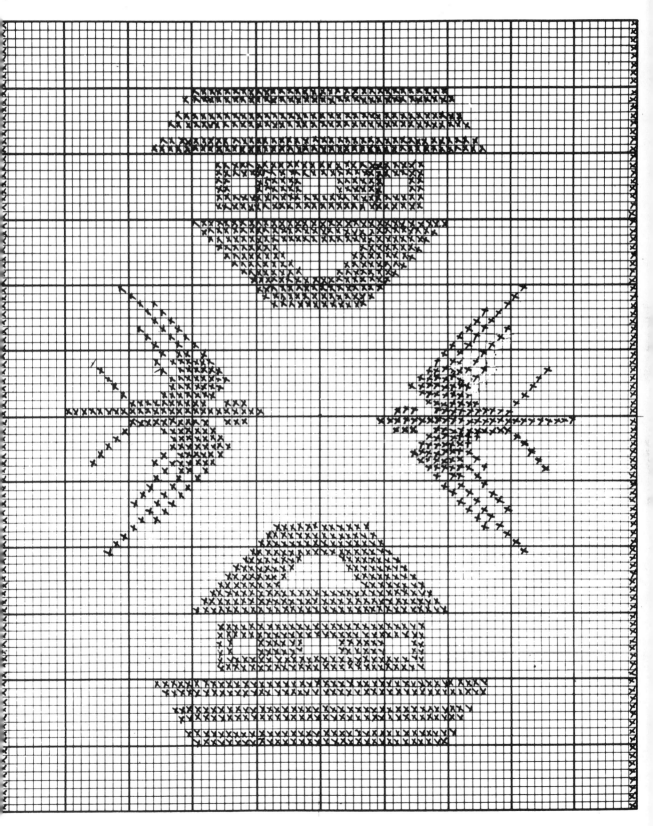

making the first row of cording at least 15 cm (6 in.) below the pins. When the work is finished with a row of knots and a fringe, the top threads can be cut and worked to match.

Double the forty threads, and hang them on the pins in the following order: 12 long, 16 short, 12 long.

The pattern
Follow the graph, working in the usual cavandoli method as described on pages 28-31, using the dark thread as pattern thread and making picots at the sides.

As it is difficult to manage the amount of pattern thread required, it could be cut into shorter lengths and added in at intervals as shown in figure 69.

To finish * Make an overhand knot over each pair of threads close to the last row of cording. Measure 7.5 cm (3 in.) from the knots and cut ends. Fray out into a fringe *.

At the beginning, cut the loops, and work from * to * to make a matching edge.

MISCELLANEOUS PATTERNS

HANGING WITH HORIZONTAL BARS, IMITATING SPRANG

(See colour plate facing page 72)

A simple and effective hanging or curtain can be knotted in imitation of a weaving technique called 'sprang', which gives a sharp, clear geometric effect. The method consists of cording across sticks (dowelling) fixed at different levels, and the knotting pattern is simply transposed threads and the occasional flat knot. The work progresses fast, and uses far less yarn than ordinary macramé.

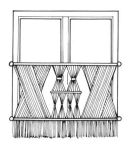

76 Ideas for using 'Sprang'

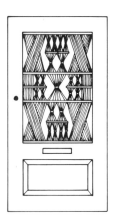

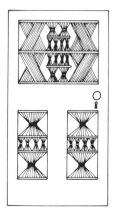

One use for this kind of quick and easy knotting is to cover large areas like windows or doors, or maybe just the glass section of doors. It can easily be adapted to all kinds of different sizes and shapes, and the ends of the sticks can be wedged in the frame of the window, or fixed in place with tiny picture tacks, or covered with a bead or wooden stopper.

A variation of this idea is to cord over plastic tubing instead of sticks. The lines will curve gently, following the natural bent of the tubing, and a curtain made this way with weaving wool looks particularly attractive in a window, where the combination of lustrous wool and transparent plastic transmutes the light to a soft glow.

The hanging in the background of colour plate 1 was made of hard, twisted weaving wool. You will need 95 m (104 yd) cut into fifty-two 180 cm (2 yd) lengths. These are doubled and set on to an 45 cm (18 in) length of thin dowelling with lark's head knots. Eight lengths of dowelling are needed, four 15 cm (6 in.) and four 45 cm (18 in.).

Work on a large board, and mark the horizontal parallel lines with lengths of black string stretched across tautly from T-pins at the sides. When cording over a length of dowelling, do not hold it in the hand but balance it on T-pins stuck into the black string each side, turning the pins so that the

Plate 3 Leather necklace with three hanging stones,
instructions page 59

Plate 4 Basket, instructions page 79
Fringes on lampshades and table, instructions
page 84
Half knot cushion, instructions page 64
Mirror with flower appliqué, instructions page 116

T is vertical and the stick cannot fall off, but there is room to work under and over it as in figure 77.

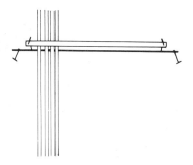

77 Working a row of horizontal cording over a rod

FIRESCREEN

This screen, for summer use in front of a fireplace, was made in wrought iron by the local blacksmith. The knotting was worked between two lengths of dowelling the exact width of the space, which were wedged into place at top and bottom, and secured with a few turns of black wire to the frame. This way of filling a frame looks neat, and is removable.

The pattern repeats in groups of 18 threads, 3 dark, 12 light, 3 dark. The dark threads are essential, but the number of light threads can be varied. Any calculation of size is governed

by the number of threads in the pattern repeat.

The screen is worked in 5 mm (^{3}/$_{16}$ in.) jute, but the same pattern in soft wools would make a good cushion.

Materials
One wrought iron frame, outer dimensions 53 cm (21 in.) wide by 63 cm (25 in.) high
Two 12 mm (½ in.) diameter lengths of dowelling to fit frame.
Homespun Jute 5 mm (^{3}/$_{16}$ in.) in two colours:
Light 124 m (136 yd)
Dark 88 m (96 yd)

Cut
Light Eight 5 yd (450 cm) lengths
Sixteen 6 yd (540 cm) lengths
Dark Eleven 8 yd (720 cm) lengths
Two 3 yd (270 cm) lengths
Two 2 ft (60 cm) lengths, for attached leaders

Set-on to a rod, with double half hitches, lengths in the following order:
One single dark 270 cm (3 yd) length
One dark 8 yd length folded 450 cm (5 yd) and 270 cm (3 yd)
*Six doubled light lengths — two 540 cm (6 yd) two 450 cm (5 yd) two 540 cm (6 yd)
One dark 720 cm (8 yd) folded 270 cm (3 yd) and 450 cm (5 yd)
One doubled dark 540 cm (6 yd) length
One dark 720 cm (8 yd) length folded 450 cm (5 yd) and 270 cm (3 yd)*

Repeat from * to * twice more

One dark 720 cm (8 yd) folded 270 cm (3 yd) and 450 cm (5 yd)
One single dark 270 cm (3 yd) length

The pattern
Each motif consists of three dark threads, twelve light threads, and three dark threads. In these groups of eighteen threads work as follows: work a row of horizontal cording with an attached leader.

1 Make a multiple flat knot with each group of light threads.

2 Cord the dark thread each side of the knot into the centre. Make double vertical half hitches into the centre over each thread with the next dark thread each side. Cord the outside dark threads into the centre.

3 In between each motif, make a multiple flat knot with the light threads.

4 Cross the motifs by using the dark threads on the right of each group as leaders, and cording them across the group of three dark threads on the left.

Continue in pattern for the desired length. Finish with a row of horizontal cording with an attached leader.

Make a double half hitch on to the second rod with each thread.

To finish Turn the ends to the back, and sew them in behind the cording. Trim. Wedge the rods in place, having spread the ends with glue. Secure the ends of the rods to the frame with wire.

SCARVES AND SHAWLS

Scarves and shawls can be made in triangular shapes which are worked on the board in a pattern of alternate flat knots, the idle threads at the sides being knotted off in every row to form a fringe.

Making a shawl is quite a project. If the prospect of making the whole thing in macramé is too much, it is always possible to make the main body of the shawl in soft fabric or machine knitting and add a macramé fringe. A fringe can pick up the colours of a patterned fabric, and can add variety to a plain one by a mixture of yarns, ribbons, beads and feathers.

Yarns The scarf in the photograph is made of fine mohair knitting yarn used double. This gives a much lighter effect than using a single thicker yarn.

Size Whether making a scarf or a shawl, decide first on the depth from the neckline to the point of the triangle (excluding the fringe). The width of the shawl will then be approximately twice this measurement.

Lengths Multiply the measurement from centre top to bottom by eight — this will be the length of the central group of threads.

Reduce the lengths working outwards from this by about 2.5 cm (1 in.) for every pair of set on threads (if you are working in doubled threads).

Technique A board large enough to take the whole piece of work is needed. Although it is quite possible to start at one corner and work across to the other, for some reason the result has an uneven look.

Set-on all the doubled threads at one time across the holding cord, with lark's head knots. If working on doubled threads, there will be four set-on threads for every flat knot instead of two. Also you will need a doubled holding cord.

Work in decreasing rows of alternate flat knots for the required length, making an overhand knot over the pairs (or four if threads are doubled) of threads left idle at the side of every row.

To finish Take the work off the board. Knot the ends of the holding cord and incorporate the ends in the fringe. Trim the fringe as described on page 84, (figure 66c).

FLOWERS

These three-dimensional shapes are made by folding a strip of cording. They can be made in all sizes, from a huge one hung on the wall, to a tiny one in metal thread worn on a ribbon round the neck. Some ideas for using these flower shapes are shown on page 102. The technique behind making flowers is an adaptation of a kind of cording called 'angling'.

Basic method of making a flower
If you are using a fine string as for the samplers, then the amount needed to make one flower will be four 4 m (4 yd) lengths.

Figure 78a Hang the lengths doubled on T-pins, and use the last thread as leader to work a row of horizontal cording from right to left.

Figure 78b Exchange the T-pins at the top of dressmaker's pins, stick a T-pin (slanting outwards) between the last two threads, and use the last thread as leader to work another row of cording, from right to left, over all threads.

Figure 78c Work two more rows of horizontal cording, using the last thread as leader. (The leader of one row becomes the last thread of the next row, as shown).

Figure 78d Turn the leader, and start cording back from left to right. Cord the first thread to the right across all the other threads for three more rows.

Figure 78e Four rows to the left and four rows to the right, results in one 'petal'. Work four more petals.

Figure 78f This strip has five petals and is now ready to be folded and sewn. Trim the ends and turn them under and sew them into the back.

Figure 78g Fold the petals as shown, sewing the central seam of each petal together, and sewing the ends together at the back. The seams can be sewn from either the front or the back, depending on the yarn, and the final appearance required.

To finish Beads can be sewn to the centre of the flower. If it is to be mounted on a strip of ribbon, or macramé, or a frame, glue it down first to a circle of leather or stiff card, to keep the shape and make it easier to apply.

Variations
Any kind of yarn can be used for these flower shapes. String will make very rigid shapes, and wool makes softer, flatter shapes.

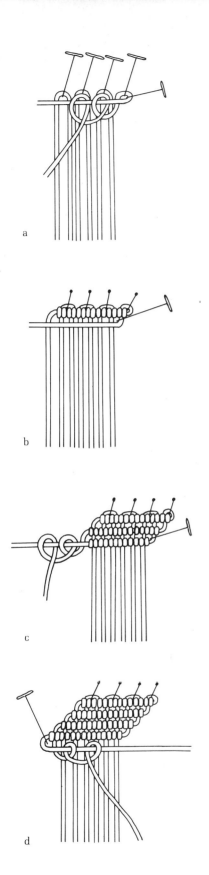

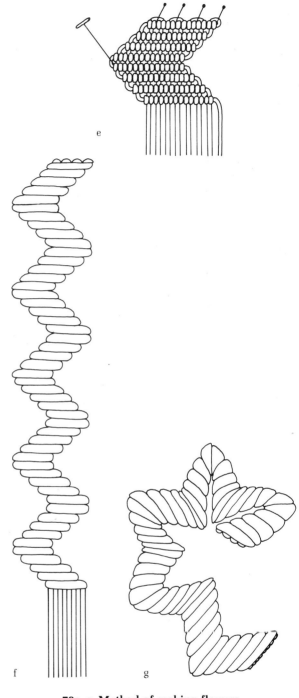

78a–g Method of making flowers

Different colours can be used. One set-on thread in a contrasting colour to the other three results in a coloured line round the flower. Flowers look attractive in four shades of one colour, arranged from light to dark.

Ideas for flowers and butterflies

More or less threads can be used, and the petals can be wider/narrower/shorter/longer. Flowers can have four, five or six petals. A single petal shape can be used separately as a leaf, or in rows as a pattern.

A strip of angling can be twisted with another strip in a different colour, like the sample in *Raffene* (see (I) on photograph on page 85) to make a braid or a bracelet.

BUTTERFLIES

Butterfly wings are a combination of angling and cording, using two colours, and incorporating beads. Like the flower shapes, wing shapes can be adapted to all sorts of other uses.

Basic method of making a butterfly wing

Materials
450 cm (5 yd) of *Twilleys Lysbet* crochet cotton in a light colour
90 cm (1 yd) in a contrasting colour

Cut
In the light colour — four 45 cm (18 in) lengths
three 90 cm (1 yd) lengths
In a contrasting colour one 90 cm (1 yd) length

Method
1 Lay the four shorter lengths of the light colour together, make an overhand knot at one end, and pin this to the board. Work a row of cording diagonally from left to right with one of the threads, as in figure 79a.

2 *Add a doubled 90 cm (1 yd) length in the light colour as follows: put a pin into the left of the work, and loop the doubled thread round it. Cord half the length over all the threads as shown in figure 79b. Take out the pin, and cord the other half over all the threads.* Repeat from * to * twice more, with the other two 90 cm (1 yd) lengths of light colour.

3 Work three more rows of cording, using the first thread as leader. (This is angling, as in figure 78c).
There should now be ten rows of cording, and ten hanging threads.

4 Use the 90 cm (1 yd) length of the contrasting colour as an attached leader, and work a row of cording across nine threads, as shown in figure 79c.

5 Make seven vertical half hitches on the tenth thread with the contrasting thread. Thread a bead on to the ninth thread. Using the tenth thread as leader, cord it back from right to left over all nine threads, as in figure 79c. The contrasting thread stays on the right, as shown.

Repeat step 5 seven more times.

6 Make a cumulative corded edge with the contrasting coloured thread as shown in figure 79d. In cumulative cording each thread corded over is added to the leader in turn, making a widening line of cording.

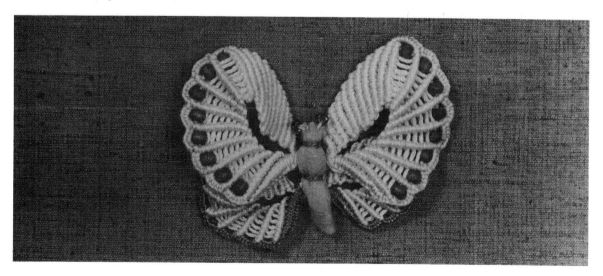

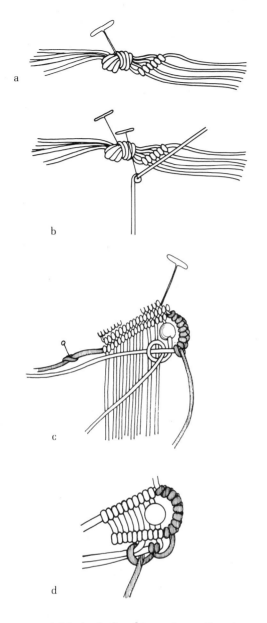

a

b

c

d

79a–d Method of making a butterfly wing

To finish Undo the overhand knot at the beginning. Fold the wings so that the beginning meets the end. Make a vertical half hitch over all threads with the contrasting thread to hold them all together. Trim all ends and sew them into the back.

Make another wing (mirror image) for the other side.

Make smaller underwings by only adding two 90 cm (1 yd) lengths instead of three, and working eight rows of cording instead of ten, and omitting the beads. Make a body out of a roll of felt, sew on the wings, add beads for eyes, and antennae of black wire.

Variations

Materials Use random coloured wool or embroidery thread for the main colour. Use marbled glass beads. Work the upper and lower wings in different colours/textures.

Design Use long narrow wings and a longer body to make a dragonfly, or shorter smaller wings and a furry body to make a bee.

Technique Make more vertical half hitches at the edges to make them frilly.

Use the angling technique (steps 1 to 4) and keep adding lengths to make triangular shapes.

Use the open cording with beads (step 5) to make frilled edgings or collars, or work in a circle to make flower shapes.

LAMPSHADES

Knotting over a frame is one of the simplest ways of making a lampshade. The pattern can be minimal, and uses an economical amount of yarn. Lampshades can be made in neutral textured yarns, and backed with a coloured or textured lining.

Yarns Lampshades need to be washable, so choose a yarn that will stand washing in a colour that is not likely to run. The other factor to be considered is whether the yarn makes a good fringe, as most lampshades are finished in this way.

Lining Nearly all macramé lampshades need a lining, as otherwise the naked bulb is visible through the knotting. This need be no more than a strip of card, grasspaper, wallpaper or stiffened fabric, cut to the depth of the frame and curled round inside, the ends lapped and held with sellotape or a touch of glue. It may be necessary to secure it to the rim at several points, but generally

this sort of lining in a drum frame keeps in place, and can be removed when the shade is washed.

The frame A drum frame, or a straight-edged frame of some sort if the easiest kind for macramé. It is recommended that tiffany frames are covered with fabric and have a macramé fringe. Curved shapes are difficult to cover, and a problem to line. A plastic-covered frame is ideal for white threads. If the frame is metal, it can either be painted to match the yarn, or covered up with knotting, ie set the threads on with double half hitches, and work the struts in very close knots.

Lengths Work one section with doubled threads which measure eight times the depth of the frame, plus the depth of the fringe. It is unlikely that threads will run out, and lengths for subsequent sections can be calculated from the amounts left over from the first one.

Doubled lengths for working the struts need to be about ten times the depth of the frame, plus the fringe allowance.

Attached leaders should be the circumference of the frame plus 15 cm (6 in.) for finishing off.

Always allow some extra length, as it is not until the work is finished that the length of the fringe can finally be decided.

Technique While work is in progress, frames can be rested on the knees, or on a table. If the pattern requires pinning to keep it symmetrical, stuff a tightly rolled length of fabric (a curtain or a towel) into the frame to act as a knotting base.

Setting-on Threads are set-on to the top rim of the frame, either with lark's head knots or double half hitches.

A doubled thread to work the struts is set-on as shown in figure 80a.

To work the top row of cording Use an attached leader. Tie it round the first strut and work across the next section. When the strut is worked, pass the leader through the knotting as shown in figure 80b.

Rings are knotted in by the following method: hold the ring in position, and cord

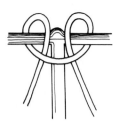

80a Setting a doubled thread on to a strut

80b Passing a leader through the knotting on a strut

four to eight threads on to the top rim with double half hitches. Pull these threads firmly, make sure the ring is in the right place, push the knots close together, figure 81. Cord the same threads on to the lower rim. Grasp the whole lot in one hand, and the ring in the other and pull the threads forwards and backwards, settling the knots on the ring and stretching the threads from top to bottom of the ring as in figure 80c.

80c Making double half hitches on the lower rim

To finish All the threads are knotted to the bottom rim with double half hitches. Those at the bottom of struts are worked as shown in figure 80c. When all the threads are on, pull them backwards and forwards, as for the ring, to make the threads taut on the frame.

The usual way of finishing a lampshade is to knot off the threads in pairs, close to the frame, and leave the ends in a fringe. Alternatively, the bottom could be finished with flat knots and beads, or groups of threads corded into V-shapes, or made into scallops with cumulative cording (figure 82) and finished with tassels.

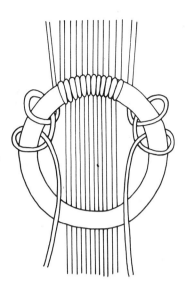

81 Incorporating a ring

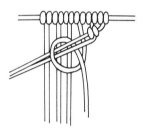

82 Cumulative cording

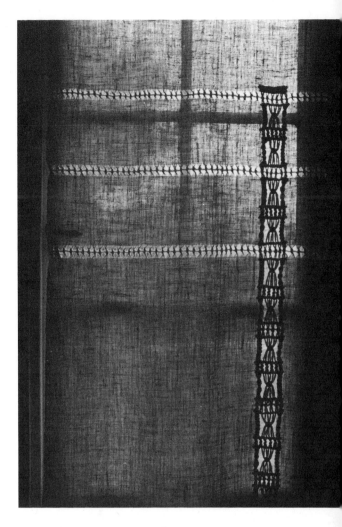

Trimming the fringe This is an important part of finishing off, as it is all too easy to finish up with an uneven edge. Work as described on page 84, but use the rolled fabric instead of a board on which to pin the work in sections.

DOOR CURTAIN

The curtain is made of off-white hessian with three horizontal drawn thread bands, and one vertical drawn thread band covered by a vertical strip of knotting.

Measurements
Curtain 200 cm x 100 cm (80 in. x 40 in.)
Macramé strip 9 cm x 127 cm (3½ in. x 50 in.)

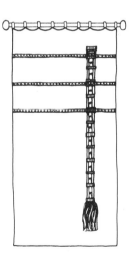

83a Door curtain

Materials
Required size of hessian for curtain 68 m
(74 yd) of 5 mm ($^3/_{16}$ in.) yarn *Bulkycord*,
or jute, or rug wool
Curtain rod
Large enough needle to take yarn

The side of the curtain with the macramé
strip is the one nearest to the hinge of the
door, and the other side is the selvedge. Turn
the fabric so that the selvedge is on the
required side according to the way your door
opens, and make a small hem across the top.

Draw the threads. The top horizontal band is
drawn first, then the wide vertical band
behind the macramé strip. The other two
horizontal bands are not drawn until the
macramé has been worked to the required
point, which will vary according to the yarn
and the tension.

Measure 30 cm (12 in.) down from the top
hem. Draw out a thread across the width of
the fabric. Measure 4 cm (1½ in.) down from
here and draw another thread out right
across. Withdraw all the threads between the
two — it will be easier if this is done in
sections.

To draw the vertical band measure 20 cm
(8 in.) from the non-selvedge edge, and withdraw a thread from the horizontal band down
to the bottom of the curtain. Withdraw
another thread 6.5 cm (2½ in.) nearer the
centre. Cut across the threads where the
vertical band meets the horizontal one and
turn under the top ends and sew or glue them
into the back of the fabric. Withdraw all the
threads between the two from the horizontal
band down to the bottom.

Macramé strip

Cut
Four 670 cm (22 ft) lengths
Four 305 cm (10 ft) lengths
Four 396 cm (13 ft) lengths

Make an overhand knot at the end of each
thread, and pin them in a row at the top of the
vertical drawn band in the following order:
* 670 cm (22 ft), 305 cm (10 ft), 670 cm (22 ft),
396 cm (13 ft), 396 cm (13 ft), 305 cm (10 ft) *

Repeat from * to * in reverse order.

1 Thread a 15 cm (6 in.) length of yarn into a

blunt thick needle, bring it up to the top
right corner of the vertical strip, and use
the yarn as an attached leader to work a
row of horizontal cording across all
threads. Take the needle through to the
back and finish off the yarn.

All the rows of horizontal cording in the
strip are worked this way, securing the
strip to the fabric.

Drop down the depth of the horizontal
drawn band and work another row of
horizontal cording in the same way.

2 *Work across drawn band* Cut a length of
yarn four times the width of the curtain,
thread into the thick needle, secure the other
end to the selvedge. Turn the curtain so that
the selvedge is at the top, the right side
facing. Take the needle under the first
bundle of twelve or so threads, pass the
needle over and under the same bundle to
the left, and then to the right through the
loop thus formed, as shown in figure 83b.

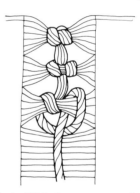

83b Double half hitches across a drawn band

This is a double half hitch, but embroiderers
will recognise it as part of a composite stitch
called raised chain band. After completing
one knot with one bundle of threads, make it
firm, and pass on to the next bundle. When
the vertical strip is reached there are no
fabric threads, but work over groups of two
macramé threads, then complete the
horizontal drawn band to the end.

3 Work a sinnet of 7 flat knots with the first
three threads. Make a flat knot over the
central two threads with a pair each side.
Make a sinnet of 7 half knots with the last
three threads.

Repeat step 1.

4 Divide the threads into pairs, and work two single knotted chains on each pair.

Repeat step 3, reversing the flat knot and half knot sinnets.

Repeat step 1.

At this point draw threads for another horizontal band the same as the first.

Drop down the depth of the band and repeat step 1, then repeat step 2.

Continue in this way, working another length of knotting and then withdrawing a third band of threads.

Work another length of knotting below this, to within 15 cm (6 in.) of the bottom of the curtain. After the final row of horizontal cording, trim the ends level with the bottom hem of the curtain.

To finish Make a hem down the cut side of the curtain. Hem across the bottom.

SHOPPING BAG
(See colour plate 1 facing page 72)

Measurements
45 cm (18 in.) wide, 30 cm (12 in.) high without handles

Materials
Topcord 4 mm (³/₁₆ in.) wide
Dark colour 96 m (104 yd) or one 100 m ball
Light colour 176 m (192 yd) or two 100 m balls
Three drive belts measuring 48 cm (19 in.) along the length, if the sides are pressed together.

Cut
For one handle, in the dark colour
Six 360 cm (4 yd) lengths
Four 405 cm (4½ yd) lengths
Two 450 cm (5 yd) lengths

To work one handle
Centre the twelve threads on the board. Use the two longest as knotting threads and work

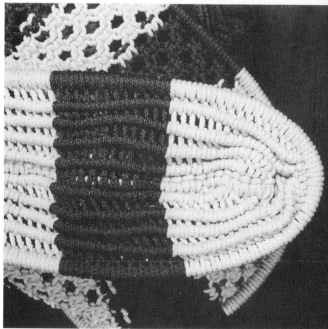

12 flat knots over all the others. Turn the work round, and with the same knotting threads work 12 flat knots the other way.

Divide the threads each end into groups of

four, two long and two short. Work 8 flat knots in each group.

Make another handle exactly the same.

A finished handle is shown in the photograph, being set-on to the belt.

To make the bag

Cut
In the light colour
Forty-eight 360 cm (4 yd) lengths

Set-on threads on to a drive belt with double half hitches as follows:
The twelve threads at one end of one handle. Six doubled light threads. The twelve threads at the other end of the same handle. Eighteen doubled light threads. Repeat from * to * once.

The pattern

1 Divide the threads into groups of twelve, keeping colour groups. Work a triple-corded diamond centred with a berry knot. Before cording the leaders back into the centre for the lower half of the diamond, loop neighbouring leaders around each other.

2 Make double half hitches with all threads over a drive belt.

3 Work in a pattern of two alternate flat knots for 18 cm (7 in.)

Repeat step 2.

The base

Figure 84a Divide the threads into two halves, front and back. Starting at the right, use the last thread as leader and cord across to the left across all the threads that side.

Figure 84b shows the end of the row. Use the next hanging thread on the right to cord across to the last thread but one on the left, as shown. Continue for four rows of cording, with about 12 mm (½ in.) or less between the rows.

Work the other side of the base in the same way. Turn the bag inside out. Make flat knots across the base by taking a thread from each side. Use a core thread or two from the centre if a thicker line is preferred.
Secure these knots by making flat knots with neighbouring ends, as shown in figure 84c.

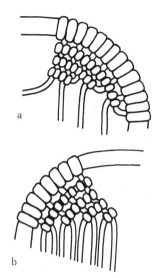

84a–b Base of shopping bag – see colour plate 1

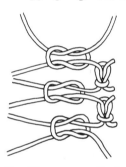

84c Knotting across the base

To finish cut all the ends close to the knotting and brush them over with rubber solution.

HESSIAN BAG WITH MACRAMÉ STRAPS AND HANDLES

Make the straps and handles before making the bag, so that everything fits, as the straps cannot be worked to an exact length.

Measurements
About 44 cm x 39 cm (17½ in. x 15½ in.) not including handles

Materials
50 cm x 85 cm (20 in. x 34 in.) of hessian, and the same amount of lining fabric
133 m (145 yd) of *Cotton Seine Twine*

Cut
Eight 825 cm (9 yd) lengths for each strap

Set-on eight doubled lengths to a short holding cord with lark's head knots. Roll each length up into a figure-of-eight bundle, secured with a rubber band, and draw out amounts as required.

To work one strap
1 Using the first thread as leader, work two rows of horizontal cording.
2 Divide the threads into groups of four and make sinnets of five half knots to the right, spiralling once.
3 Using the last thread as leader, work two rows of horizontal cording.
4 Make a sinnet of five flat knots on the first and last groups of four threads. Make one flat knot with pairs of knotting threads with the central eight threads.

Repeat step 1.

5 Divide the threads into groups of four and make sinnets of five half knots to the left, spiralling once.

Repeat step 3.

Continue in pattern, using the first and last threads alternately as leaders for the rows of horizontal cording, until the work measures about 75 cm (30 in.). Finish on a pattern matching the start of the strap.

Work the handle as follows: * make a sinnet of four flat knots on the first four threads, the centre eight threads, and the last four threads.* Group all the threads together, and using the two longest as knotting threads work about 25 cm (10 in.) of flat knots. Work from * to * once more. Cut the ends about 7.5 cm (3 in.) below the last knots.

Work another strap with the handle exactly the same.

To make up the bag
Fold the hessian in half and sew up the sides. Turn right way out again and press. Fold in 2.5 cm (1 in.) round the top for a hem and pin. Lay the bag flat and mark the position of the straps with chalk lines, making sure they are parallel with each other and with the sides.

Looking at the bag as it is in the photograph, pin the free end of one handle behind the top of the strap marks on the right. Move left for the width of the handle and pin the other end to the top of the other strap marks. Pin the strap down this left side, under the bag, and up the other side. Pin the free end of the other handle behind this end, move across the width of the handle, pin the other end of it in place, then pin the strap down the bag, under it, and up to finish where you began with the first handle. Adjust the handles,

straps and the depth of the hem at the top of the bag until everything fits.

Machine across the loose threads at the free ends of the handles through the hem at the top of the bag — this will be covered by the set-on end of the other strap — and sew down the straps with matching buttonhole twine and a chenille needle.

Make a lining in the same way as the bag, fit it inside, and hem round the top.

HANDLES FOR A SEMI-CIRCULAR RUSH BASKET

As this kind of basket has a large capacity, the handles often wear out before the basket, and this braid acts both as handles and an extra support to the woven straw. Thick jute is used because it is comfortable for a handle

and does not cut into the straw. A long braid, almost 270 cm (3 yd) is knotted, and sewn on to the basket in one continuous length, joined at the bottom.

Measurements
Basket 30 cm (1 ft) high, about 63 cm (25 in.) across
Braid about 270 cm (3 yd) long

Materials
48 m (53 yd) of *Homespun Jute* 4 mm (³/₁₆ in.) wide

Cut
Cut one 630 cm (7 yd) length
Two 21 m (23 yd) lengths

Set-on doubled to a short holding cord, with lark's head knots, the shortest length in the centre.
Roll up the outer lengths in figure-of-eight hanks, secure them with rubber bands, and draw out lengths as required.

The pattern
Work a pattern of alternate lark's head knots as shown in figure 85, until the yarn is used up. Finish with a line of horizontal cording, and trim the ends.

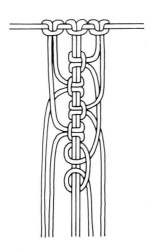

85 Alternate lark's head braid

To make up Arrange the braid on the basket as shown in the photograph, lapping the ends slightly underneath the basket. Sew the braid down with matching twine, catching down the threads at each side every 2.5 cm (1 in.) or

so, and leaving the long stitches at the back. If it is sewn too tightly it may cut the fabric, so keep the stitching easy. If the braid slips on the bag, keep it in place with sellotape until it is sewn down. Lap the ends at the bottom and sew them together.

SHOULDER BAG WITH INITIALLED FLAP

(See colour plate 1 facing page 72)

Measurements
30 cm wide x 22 cm high x 5 cm deep
(12 in. wide x 9 in. high x 2 in. deep)

Materials
Country Jute — 3 mm (⅛ in.) wide in off-white with contrasting initials and edging
Off-white 262 m (286 yd)
Contrasting colour about 11 m (12 yd)

The body of the bag is worked in a pattern of alternate flat knots, with a section of horizontal cording across the base and the top. The flap is in cavandoli work incorporating a pattern of initials. The strap starts at the centre shoulder with rows of cording, followed by a length of alternate flat knots, the last 22 cm (9 in.) of which are worked down the sides of the bag as gussets.

Cut
In off-white
Twelve 405 cm (4½ yd) lengths
Eighteen 450 cm (5 yd) lengths
One 225 cm (2½ yd) length
One 405 cm (4½ yd) length
Two 60 cm (2 ft) lengths

Set-on to a 60 cm (2 ft) holding cord, with lark's head knots, doubled threads in the following order: six 405 cm (4½ yd) lengths, Eighteen 450 cm (5 yd) lengths, six 405 cm (4½ yd) lengths.

The pattern
For the main part of the bag.
1 Work one row of horizontal cording with an attached 60 cm (2 ft) leader
2 Work 20 cm (8 in.) of alternate flat knots
3 Using the 225 cm (2½ yd) length as an attached leader, work six rows of horizontal cording.

Repeat step 2.

4 Using the 405 cm (4½ yd) length as an attached leader, work ten rows of horizontal cording.

The flap

Cut in the contrasting colour—
One 720 cm (8 yd) length
Two 180 cm (2 yd) lengths

Use the long contrasting pattern thread, and start to work the cavandoli graph at the top line of vertical half hitches. Work five more rows, turning the thread at the sides in the usual way but not pinning it out to make picots. Squares are marked on the graph for up to three initials. Fit the chosen letters into the appropriate spaces. Start the top line of the pattern in the next row.

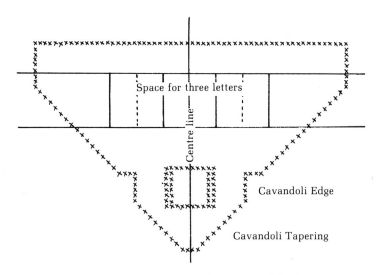

87a Graph for cavandoli flap to shoulder bag

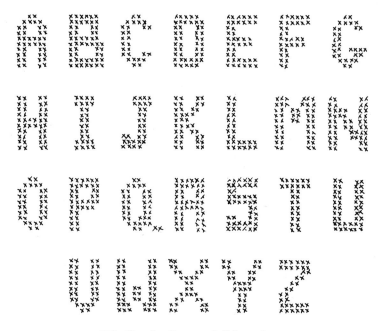

87b Graph of cavandoli lettering

After the eighth row from the top of the graph, taper the flap by leaving an idle thread at the beginning and end of each row for the next 16 rows, and omitting the vertical half hitched edge. When the end of this section is reached, attach a 180 cm (2 yd) length each side at the start of the section, and work a cumulative corded edge down each side. Leave the ends and the contrasting lengths idle, to be sewn into the back afterwards.

The next straight section is cavandoli work without picots, and the last section is tapered but still with the cavandoli edge, worked as shown for the tapered end of the watch strap on page 88.

At the bottom turn the last few ends under and sew them into the back.

The strap

Cut in off-white
Eleven 10 m (11 yd) lengths
One 11 m (12 yd) length

Centre the lengths on the board. Using the longest one as leader, work 18 rows of horizontal cording from the centre. Turn the work round, and with the same leader work another 18 rows in the opposite direction.

From each end of the strap, work 38 cm (15 in.) of alternate flat knots, finishing with three rows of horizontal cording.

To knot the strap to the bag Fold the bag so that the holding cord is level with the lowest row of the central group of cording. Lay the

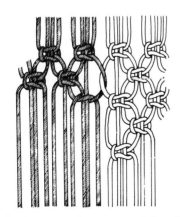

86 Incorporating a strap into a bag

strap in position so that the last row of cording is level with the cording on each side. Pin in place on the board. Pass the first and last threads of the strap through the flat knot loops at the sides of the bag as shown in figure 86. Work in alternate flat knots the depth of the gusset, passing the threads each side of the strap through the knotting on the bag every alternate row. At the bottom, pull all the ends of the strap through from the front to back with a crochet hook. Sew the ends inside and trim.

'PETAL' FRAME

Measurements
33 cm (13 in.) diameter

Materials
56 m (61 yd) of *Rayon Cord* 3 mm (⅛ in.) wide
5.5 m (6 yd) of coloured yarn, 3 mm (⅛ in.) wide
One lampshade ring 20 cm (8 in.) diameter

The cord used for this frame was white, and the lampshade ring was covered in white plastic. If a coloured yarn is used, either paint the ring to match, or set the threads on with double half hitches so that the ring does not show.

Cut in white cord
Seventy-two 75 cm (2½ ft) lengths
One 1 m (1 yd) length for an attached leader.

The pattern for one petal
Set-on twelve doubled 75 cm (2½ ft) lengths to the ring.

1 Using the attached leader, make a row of horizontal cording across all threads.

2 Using the attached coloured yarn as leader, make a vertical double half hitch on each thread.

3 Work six diminishing rows of alternate flat knots, leaving two threads idle at the beginning and end of every row after the first.

4 Cord the first and last thread into the centre, crossing them where they meet. Repeat once.

5 Make an overhand knot over the two centre
  threads. Cut all ends about 12 mm (½ in.)
  from the cording, and fray them out.

To finish Sew in the ends of the attached
leaders.

This frame could be mounted over a round
mirror, or used as a picture or photo frame.
The petal edge could be used in soft wool to
trim a round cushion.

Tiny versions of this pattern worked in fine
crochet thread on curtain rings or wire will
make little flower shapes.

NOTES ON YARNS

Where a yarn specified in this book is not available the following descriptions may help in locating a similar product.

Bulkycord (Atlascraft) 4-5 mm (³/₁₆ in.) Top Knot (Tweedy Products) Multicraft Yarn (Dunlicraft)	A soft synthetic yarn, similar to rug wool
Cotton Seine Twine (Atlascraft) Dunlicrame (Dunlicraft) 1.5 mm (¹/₁₆ in.)	A smooth twisted string
Jute — available in 2-6 ply, and in different widths (Atlascraft) 2-3 mm (¹/₁₆ in.-⅛ in.) 'Natural', 2.5-3 mm (⅛ in.-³/₁₆ in.) 'Country', 4-5 mm (³/₁₆ in.) 'Homespun'	The natural fibre of the jute plant
Lustrecord (Atlascraft) 2 mm (¹/₁₆ in.)	A unique crunchy metallic yarn, a synthetic core wrapped with a metallized thread
Maxicord (Impex) 10 mm (⅜ in.)	A thick bulky synthetic fibre
Novacord (Atlascraft) 2.5 mm (⅛ in.)	A tubular knitted yarn with a crunchy finish
Raffene (Atlascraft) Craftene (Dunlicraft)	Synthetic dyed raffia
Patons Turkey Rug Wool 6 mm (¼ in.)	Pure wool yarn
Rayon Cord (Atlascraft) Mini Cord (Impex) Nylon cord (Johnson Aldridge)	A hard twisted yarn with a lustrous finish
Schurer SI	Fine metal sewing thread
Suisses Weekend Wool	Chunky knitting wool, thicker than double double
Topcord (Atlascraft) 4 mm (³/₁₆ in.) Craft cord (Impex) Marcord (Johnson Aldridge)	Braided nylon
Tubular Rayon Cord (Atlascraft) 2 mm (¹/₁₆ in.)	A knitted tubular yarn
Twilleys Lysbet and Crysette	Mercerised Crochet cottons 5 and 3

SUPPLIERS

Campden Needlecraft Centre
High Street   Chipping Campden
Gloucestershire

Cuckoo Craft Supplies
23 Kings Road   Reading   Berkshire

de Denne Ltd
159/161 Kenton Road
Kenton   Harrow   Middlesex

General Crafts Ltd
PO Box 33   Harrow   Middlesex
(mail order for Maxicord)

Heritage Crafts
76 Wey Hill   Haslemere   Surrey

Hobby Horse
15/17 Langton Street
London SW10

Leisurecrafts Centre
2-10 Jerdan Place   London SW6 5PT

Lewiscraft
27 The Merrion Centre   Leeds

Leven Crafts and Hobbies
54 Church Square
Guisborough   Cleveland

The Needlecraft Shop
Smallgate   Station Road
Beccles   Suffolk

Wools and Embroideries
3/5 Queens Parade   Hendon Central
London NW4 3AR
(mail order for Patons Rug Wool)

BIBLIOGRAPHY

ASHLEY, Clifford W *The Ashley Book of Knots,* Faber and Faber Ltd, London

HARVEY, Virginia I *Colour and Design in Macramé* Van Nostrand Reinhold Co, New York/London

HARVEY, Virginia I *Macramé: the art of creative knotting* Reinhold Publishing Corporation, New York

SCHMID-BURLESON, Bonny *The Technique of Macramé* B.T. Batsford Ltd, London Charles T. Branford Co, Newton Centre, Massachusetts

SHORT, Eirian *Introducing Macramé* B.T. Batsford Ltd, London, Watson-Guptill Publications, New York

INDEX